CHILE·

CONVERSATIONS WITH WINEMAKERS

Grape Collective

Grape Collective Publishing
A division of Grape Collective
2669 Broadway, New York, NY 10025

Edited by Christopher Barnes
Interviews by Christopher Barnes
Copyright © 2016 Grape Collective

CHILE

CONTENTS

ACKNOWLEDGMENTS

While the title is Conversations with Winemakers, the focus of this book is to interview people who are part of a region's wine story, and this includes winery owners and industry insiders. During our trip to Chile, the passionate winemakers and owners who I spoke with were very giving of their time and very honest in their assessments about the challenges and opportunities facing the Chilean wine industry.

Many people helped to create this book. Thank you to Monty Waldin, Derek Mossman Knapp and Amanda Barnes for their advice during the planning of the trip. Thanks go to the winemakers of Chile who were so giving of their time. Special thanks to Alfonso Nogueroles, my partner in this project for traveling across the world to film the thoughts and experience of Chile's winemakers. Piers Parlett, Bruce Kuo and Christopher Sabatini for their design input. Barbara Vyden and Rachael Doob for their help in proofreading. Lastly, I'm grateful for the wonderful energy provided by the team of writers contributing to Grape Collective who make the project fun to be a part of.

AN INTRODUCTION TO
Chile

Chile is blessed with the ideal geography, geology and climate to produce wines that are both distinctive and outstanding. Rich in natural beauty and vast wilderness, the country occupies a long narrow strip at the very tip of South America. Its natural borders are protected by the Pacific Ocean to the west, the Andes Mountains to the east, the Atacama Desert to the north and Patagonia to the south. Its climate is similar to California - sunny and dry with a short rainy season. During grape growing season the days are warm and the nights cool Importantly, due to its natural barriers, the vine eating louse phylloxera has not found its way to Chile, meaning that the older vines remain healthy and ungrafted.

Grape growing arrived with the Spanish conquistadors in the 1500s. The early grapes were very likely the País or Mission grapes from Spain or the Canary Islands. Today Chile has become a highly export-focused market. In the mid-19th century, French wine varietals such as Cabernet Sauvignon, Merlot, Carménère and Cabernet Franc were planted. A further winemaking advance occurred in the early 1980s, with the introduction of stainless steel fermentation tanks and the use of oak barrels for aging.

Chile has many unique wine regions with distinct terroir. For a while the Chilean wine community debated as to whether Chile should stand behind a particular grape varietal much in the way Argentina has become closely affiliated with Malbec. Carménère and Cabernet Sauvignon were the two varietals held up as potential flag bearers. However that movement seems to have faded and now the theme seems to be focusing on the great diversity of Chile's terroir.

From the Atacama dessert in the north, to Bío Bío in the south, each region has its own unique personality and grapes that thrive. The

Casablanca Valley by the coast is cool and foggy - perfect for Pinot Noir and Sauvignon Blanc; Maipo and Colchuago in central Chile have hotter days and are best suited to big hearty reds such as Cabernet and Carménère. Maule, to the south of Maipo, focuses primarily on Cabernet and Carignan. Bío Bío and Itata to the far south have a cool Mediterranean climate that befits País, Muscat and Carignan vines.

In the US, Chilean wines are firmly established in the value category. A major challenge for the industry has been that it is dominated by three major wineries; Concha Y Toro, Santa Rita and San Pedro (VSPT) together sell 80 percent of Chilean wines. The 1990s saw a wine boom in Chile that attracted major international investment including the Rothschilds of Bordeaux's Chateaux Lafite (Los Vascos), Alexandra Marnier Lapostolle of Grand Marnier (Casa Lapostolle), Miguel Torres from Spain and America's Jackson Family Wines (Calina).

If there is a wine hero in Chile it is Aurelio Montes. Montes is the self-made man in an industry dominated by privilege and big conglomerates. He was the first to bang the drum internationally about the quality wines being produced. He used innovative marketing including enlisting the iconoclastic artist Ralph Steadman to design the bottle

labels. On every bottle of Montes wine it says "From Chile with Pride."

Today a new wave of small dedicated artisan producers is elevating the wine reputation of the country. Organizations like MOVI (Movimiento de Viñateros Independientes, the Movement of Independent Vintners in English) and VIGNO (a movement dedicated to promoting old vine Carignan) have emerged, helping the small producers speak with a louder voice. The purpose of these organizations is to promote small and quality-oriented wineries that make wine personally, on a human scale. It is a story that is slowly starting to find resonance internationally, as it is certainly much more interesting to engage with Chile's wine Davids rather than the corporate Goliaths.

DEREK MOSSMAN KNAPP
GARAGE WINE CO.

Derek Mossman Knapp stands out amongst his fellow Chilean winemakers. An exuberant Canadian who first came to Chile to ski, he has managed to insert himself into the heart of Chile's vibrant artisanal wine movement. Mossman Knapp is one of the founding members of MOVI, the Movement for Independent Vintners, an organization of small artisanal producers who have managed to garner international attention for Chile's emerging boutique wine industry. He started the Garage Wine Company as a hobby in 2001 in collaboration with his wife Pilar Miranda and their friend, Dr. Alvaro Peña.

We talk to Mossman Knapp about the great potential of Chile's old vines and his journey to become a Chilean winemaker.

Christopher Barnes: So Derek you're from Canada. How does someone from Toronto end up in Maule making wine?

Derek Mossman Knapp: I came here to ski in a year when I was originally supposed to go to New Zealand, but it didn't snow there. So I was out of a summer job and I came to Chile instead, and it grew on me. I came back and it was my summer job during my years at university.

A lot of people have summer jobs but very few people stay and become part of the fabric of the country that they adopt or that adopts them. What was it about Chile that tugged at your heart and made you take root?

I think wine is a good piece of it. I also met a winemaker and married a Chilean. That probably closed the deal.

Love is always a good reason, right?

Absolutely.

And how did you get involved in the wine business?

We began with friends goofing around in the garage. And it was never intended to grow into something more than a few barrels to enjoy with family and friends. One thing led to the next and it was always just over the next hill that there's something more intriguing, there's another fruit, another something, and it just got the best of us.

Derek, tell us about this vineyard in Maule.

This is Nivaldo's vineyard, near Sauzal. This is the cooler extreme of Maule.

What sort of grapes are planted here?

Originally, this was a País vineyard with some old Carignan. We extended the Carignan and put a little bit of Garnacha on the hill behind us here to have the first shade of the afternoon. We put a little bit of Mataró (Mourvèdre), with a little more water in the bottom of the hill.

And how old are the vines?

This would literally be colonial root stock. There would be plants that are 150 to 200 or even more years old.

How does the age of the vines reflect in the taste of the wine that you make?

There's definitely a complexity factor in the age of the vines. But, these vines have been done with Mugron, where you take one chute that's not pruned and create a new plant to have greater density. These vineyards have never been replanted, but they've always been continuously filled in and balanced out. So you'd have a balance of some plants 15 years old and some plants that would be 150 years old.

When did you decide to transition from the garage and turn into a real full-fledged business, become an entrepreneur, make, sell and market wine, and all the things that go with running a business?

Every time we were frustrated that it was starting to put a dent in family finances, thinking that we can't keep doing this anymore, something out of the blue would happen, and that was a sign that we had to take this to the next level. What got us out of the garage and starting to export was when we met other people like us and formed MOVI.

Tell us about MOVI.

MOVI initially was a buying group. For example, if you made 5,000 or 6,000 bottles of wine, the bottle makers didn't know how to deliver to you because you didn't have a forklift. The capsule makers didn't know how to organize an order for less than 15,000 or 20,000. The corks were even more complicated. So we came together in the hope that they would answer an email, give us a quote, and want to do business with us.

And, when did you start MOVI?

We started MOVI six or seven years ago now. The years have flown by. And after we formed and realized there was a real camaraderie, and things to be learned from each other, we were invited to take our wines to a tasting at a London wine fair. And the world liked our wines.

Talk a little bit about the types of winemakers that make up MOVI.

In MOVI there's a wide selection. There are a few outsiders, there's a Canadian, a Swiss lawyer, an Italian count from Tuscany, but mostly they are family projects, kind of very personal projects with a great deal of volition of winemakers who either still work in a big company and have a forward-thinking boss, or who definitively left said big company and want to have an entrepreneurial experience on their own.

What types of wines are the MOVI winemakers making?

You could divide MOVI into three flights. You have relatively new things that have been planted in the last 15 years which would be a lot of Syrah, Pinot Noir, and Sauvignon Blanc probably close to the coast of whatever valley it's in. We also have some of the classics, but rethought or reloaded, which would be Aconcagua and Maipo but now made with a personal twist. We say in the Maule that the old is the new new, which would be old vine varieties that probably haven't been appreciated in or associated with Chile in many years, such as Carignan, Torontel and Tempranillo.

Is there a shared philosophy of winemaking behind these winemakers?

It would be very hard to typify a MOVI wine. They're very different. I

think there is a certain element of going back to the roots. I would say it's anti-technological, but it's definitely moving towards letting the earth express itself by not getting in the way. The work is done in the vineyard and the rest is done by hand.

What is the volume of MOVI winemaking - small, large, average?

Garage today makes a little more than 3,000 cases and we'd probably be considered mid-size. We have some smaller MOVI winemakers who make about 1,000 cases. And the largest MOVI winemakers are making 10,000, and one is even approaching 20,000. But, it's really not a size issue, it's how personally involved the owner is with the making of the wine.

Internationally, Chile is known for its very large companies like

Concha Y Toro, that produce good quality wine at a very, very low price point. How does MOVI get the word out about the interesting things that it's doing here?

People tell me that they're happy to taste and I get the sense that Chile has kind of a debt to the world. They literally ask me, "Where have they been hiding you?" The developed markets, the wine markets of the world, love a good David and Goliath story. They like things that are very personal. They've had a lot of commodities - food, cars, shirts, shoes - in their life to last more than a lifetime. When things go back to basics, and to the old ways and are more personal, is when volitional people zone right in.

Derek, what does MOVI mean? What is the acronym MOVI?

MOVI is the Movimiento de Viñateros Independientes. The Movement of Independent Vintners sounds much more Monty Python in Spanish than it does in English. It's a little tongue-in-cheek humor referencing Chile's political history and viñatero, which is a landed family who besides its large construction holdings, obviously also has a vineyard.

Which is sort of funny, because everyone is very small and family oriented.

Absolutely.

Derek, you started the Garage Wine Company. Is that like Steve Jobs starting out in his garage? Are you going to be Constellation one day?

No. I'll never be Constellation. I celebrate the fact that we began in the garage. I don't see an association with "Garagistes" of St. Émilion who made over-done wines in my way of thinking. I think it's a tremendous testament in many businesses to have to roll out that car to have some working space in the garage. To get some things done this afternoon we physically began in the garage and once the name was coined, there was no going back. A magazine article came out and that's what they called it; it was too late to change it later.

When did you start the Garage Wine Company?

2001 was when we began tinkering in the garage. In 2006 we started thinking more about how we get exports going, et cetera. And the last three or four years we've grown to a little more than 3,000 cases in 14 countries.

Derek your approach is very artisanal. How do you find these old vines that you use to make your wines?

To me, the experience after the earthquake was when we had the opportunity to help some people through kind of our own, how do you say, bootstrapping program. It was like putting a backpack back on, except I was in an old red truck and I was thinking that just over the next hill there's something that's just kick-ass that no one is paying attention to. And somewhere there is someone who can benefit from it, because we can take their grapes that today are making jug wine and being paid a trifle, and we can turn it into fine wine for export, and pay them a solid price that they know they'll always have.

Fantastic. Tell me about the different varietals you make at the Garage Wine Company.

From the very beginning, we have been making a Cabernet Sauvignon blend from the Maipo, and we also make a Cabernet Franc pure varietal from the Maipo, and then in Maule we make wines in seven sites. And the varieties we include would be Garnacha, Tempranillo, Mataró, País, Carignan.

On your label each wine has a lot number on it. How does that work?

From day one, or lot one, we have always put a lot number on it. And it complicated some of the importers because it would change and we said no, no this isn't a marketing concept. Every lot we make will have a number. Some people still remember all the way back to number five. I remember it was Cabernet but I can't really place the tasting notes in my head. We're now at lot 51 and we're bottling next week.

And do different lots go to different countries? I mean, how different are the taste profiles of the different lots you produce?

In the Maule wines there are definite properties because they have more herbs and spices in the soil in between the plants. They have a funkier tone, and there are markets that like that more than other wines. I think it's very important that if Chile has been seen as being, how do you say, marching to almost a military march, I think we have to learn some syncopation. I think we need to insert some jazz. I think we have to break up the rhythm, break up the step and do some things that are unexpected and open minds to what Chile could be doing.

And how has the Garage Wine Company evolved since you started?

We've changed things, but we are the three original partners - me, my wife Pilar, and Dr. Alvaro Peña from the University of Chile. And I think what has not evolved, or what has not changed is the intrigue of experimentation. We began making wine in 500-kilo plastic bins and we could separate things to compare and contrast and we continue to do that to this day. Eight, nine barrels or 18 barrels and we never mix them before we bottle. So you have a whole series of permutations of how it was treated, how it was done, what barrel it was in, what battonage it had. In the end, only about two or three days before it is bottled, do you ever combine them. I think that creates a complexity and I hope we never change. I hope that curiosity never goes away.

Derek, how do you see some of the challenges facing the Chilean wine industry at the moment?

I think the biggest challenge in the Chilean wine industry today is comfort. People are in a zone and they're comfortable; they have to get out of the comfort zone. In the end, we have this baseline of products that people know to be tried and true at a certain price point. And then we have these, I'm not sure they're egotistical or what, they are project or icon wines and I don't think it's sustainable to have these too. I think it's between 20 and 35 dollars where Chile can just rock the house. And that's where MOVI has done well and I think the world wants more of those wines. I think where Chile has to start concentrating more, is in the middle. Its not a question of how much you can charge for the wine, it's getting people to try new things and to think of Mediterranean varieties and to think of wines from the north and to think of things radically close to the coast. I think Chile can do all of that.

A lot of people talk about Chile standing behind one grape, be it Carménère or Cabernet Sauvignon, in the same way that Argentina is very much associated with Malbec. Do you feel that Chile needs a grape to stand behind, or do you see that Chile has to be about diversity?

Years ago a Canadian prime minister spoke of the cultural mosaic. I think mosaic is the term for Chile's wine country. Diversity is just another word for indecision. Chile is this tremendous mosaic of terroir and I think we have to learn to separate and become comfortable. Let's do a vintage report or an analysis or a wine tasting of these and let's separate those.

In terms of the viticulture in the vineyards that you source your grapes, is there something unique you do there?

I think it's getting back to old ways of letting people work with horses as they used to do, but combining that with information, or a lens that science can provide to help guide us a little more. If wines reduce in

the cellar, let's think about what the change in compost is for next year instead of compensating chemically. Let's think long term, but let's use the old methods but with some better preparation and some better knowledge of why this is happening.

Tell me a little more about Maule. What is the terroir like in this region?

Maule is very diverse, just like Chile. We are here in the beginning of the coastal range with granitic soils, more crystals in the soil, and different rock structure. Because of the mountains and slower cooling, there's bedrock beneath the soils that roots can get into. And I think that changes the flavor in the wines.

www.garagewineco.cl

MOVI

If you are a small artisanal winemaker in an emerging wine region how do you get the world to notice your wines? And for the emerging wine region as a whole, how do you promote your artisan winemakers to the rest of the world? The invention of MOVI (Movimiento de Viñateros Independientes - the Movement of Independent Vintners in English) in Chile is a model that answers both of these questions.

MOVI is a group of independent Chilean winemakers who banded together in 2009 to form a purchasing group and marketing organization. There are 24 winemakers who produce between several thousand to 15,000 cases per year. The organization allows small family producers to find a voice and get their wines tasted internationally by critics and importers. The qualifications for membership of MOVI is to be small and quality oriented, and to make wine on a human scale. The focus of the organization is very much about building community - and each new member invites the other members to their winery.

For wine lovers who want to support small family wineries the challenge is that those businesses often don't have the resources to manage marketing, nor do they have the sales expertise to allow their wines to be available outside their local market. For a country like Chile which is known internationally for budget wines, MOVI is a breath of fresh air - an artisanal movement that people can get excited about.

MOVI was created from a practical standpoint to help small winemakers create a buying group to purchase bottles, corks, labels and other winemaking equipment in a country which is dominated by three massive winemaking entities such as Concho Y Toro (which according to The Drinks Business is now the largest winery in the world), Santa Rita and VSPT, which together sell four out of five bottles of Chilean wine. Since its inception, marketing has become the key value driver of the organization. Critics such as the Financial Times columnist Jancis Robinson, Alder Yarrow and the Wine Spectator have reviewed the wines of small family producers who on their own would struggle to get even local recognition.

Following MOVI is the growth of Vigno (Vignadores de Carignan) an organization aimed at promoting old vine Carignan. The Vigno criteria is that winemakers must be mostly Carignan based, utilize vines that are at least 30 years of age and dry farm.

There is a sense of fun and adventure about MOVI. The members all originate from different parts of the country with very different backgrounds which include lawyers, doctors, ex-pat miners and an Italian count; but they all seem to enjoy the camaraderie and the connectedness that MOVI brings to them. Jancis Robinson captured this in a recent column. "The MOVI and VIGNO crew are a cheeky lot and have clearly enjoyed cocking a snook at the old guard of Chilean wine, which makes it all the more remarkable that there has been such a rush to copy them from precisely the big companies that they set out to shake."

MOVI is an important addition to the overall Chilean wine industry. There is something very underdog about them in a country where the big dog is very dominant. How can a wine lover not embrace passionate family winemakers making heartfelt artisanal wines from old vines? Now compare the story of the mass produced industrial "value" wines - which is sexier, David or Goliath? When we met with Chilean wine pioneer and President of Wines of Chile, Aurelio Montes, he was glowing in his praise of MOVI. While they are not fee paying members of Wines of Chile, Montes was keen to point out that they are invited to press events as their story is an important part of the narrative of modern Chilean wine.

Amongst the MOVI members there is a diversity in style and geography from the far south to the Atacama Desert in the north. The common link among members is the passion of the people producing the wines and their shared ambition to raise the profile of quality winemaking in Chile. Chile has some wonderful natural assets including some of the world's oldest ungrafted vines. A country protected by the Andes, Pacific Ocean, Atacama Desert and Patagonia, it has never suffered from the vine destroying louse phylloxera. Vines have been discovered that are 300 years old.

The wines are interesting, full of passion and life. We spoke to some of

the MOVI members about what it means to be MOVI.

Angelica Grove and Andrés Costa, Rukumilla Wines

Angelica and Andrés started Rukumilla as a small private wine company in 2004. They produce about 2,000 bottles a year organically in Maipo in the southern part of Santiago.

Their main business is selling stainless steel wine tanks in the United States, Europe, Australia and New Zealand.

Andrés Costa: I think MOVI is an exceptional group. We are the founders of MOVI. This organization was founded in 2006, with 12 members, and now we are 24. I think it is the only way to show others the way we produce wines, because we don't have the resources to create big advertising or big promotional events. The idea is to help all the small vineyards and producers to show our work, our passion, and also to show another face of the Chilean market, not just the big wineries. I'm very proud to be part of MOVI. We think that this kind of association helps a lot in the wine industry to show a different face.

Angela Mochi, Sucre and Tunquen

Angela and her husband Marcos are Brazilians who built a successful wine import company in their native Brazil and then decided to leave it all, go off the grid, and move to a coastal area of Chile. Their water comes from a well and is pumped through solar panels using solar energy. They use refurbished shipping containers because they are isolated and don't need to use power from the grid to keep the wines

at a perfect temperature. They make two ranges of wines: Sucre wines which are produced using mainly Cabernet and Carménère, and Tunquen wines which are predominantly Malbec, Cabernet Franc, Syrah, Pinot Noir and Sauvignon Blanc.

Christopher Barnes: Angela, you're one of the directors of MOVI.

Angela Mochi: MOVI is an organization, today we are 24 producers, but we're growing and we're just small family businesses. We are people who are fully involved, not just making the wines but commercializing the wine as well. So there are no big corporations in MOVI, we are just small companies making everything. The first time I heard about MOVI, I was still living in Brazil and it just made perfect sense for us to join MOVI because in some way, what we are doing is what the others are doing, and so when we join together we are 24, we have much more strength together than we have when we are apart. That is what MOVI does best. We have a voice, through MOVI, a voice that we could never ever have if we were alone by ourselves. MOVI gives us that voice and we can talk to the world through MOVI.

And what does MOVI stand for?

There's one simple, really simple phrase that says that we dare to think small. We're thinking small, we're not thinking big. We are mainly family businesses, so there are people making 200 cases, and there are people making 15,000 cases, but they are all family businesses and thinking small. This goes against practically everything that you ever heard, because people in general teach you to think big. No, we

are challenging that. We are thinking small, and doing what we can to do the best for our families, and all the families in MOVI.

Fernando Atabales, Starry Night Vineyard

Fernando is a medical doctor who bought a house which came with some Syrah and Pinot Noir vines. The property is at the edge of Maipo and located at the start of the Casablanca Valley. He fell in love with winemaking and makes wines with the help of his extended family. The vineyard is their garden.

Christopher Barnes: How did you get involved with MOVI and what does MOVI mean?

Fernando Atabales: MOVI is a movement of independent vineyards, it's like the Vigneron in France, but little because we are only 22 or 23 people. Each one of us makes his wines and is involved in all the processes, all the processes of the wine with his or her family, depending. And normally we make the wines that we want to drink. And we are trying to show the place and the style of wine we want to drink everyday in our house, with our friends. So if people like that, it's better, but normally we are trying to show that, so we have produced a very small amount of wines. We produce about 5,000 bottles of Syrah and 3,000 bottles of Pinot Noir, and that's all every year. And the other partners are similar, from 1,000 cases, to I don't know, maybe 5,000 cases, for the biggest one of us.

Normally all of us are involved in the wines, in the selection of the grapes, in the process of the wine, in the control of fermentation, in the palate of the wine, in deciding what kind of barrel to use or if no barrel should be used, or what kind of process for fermentations, and the bottles and the labels and everything. From the little ones putting labels on bottles to the older ones, the whole family is working harder, I think. But I think it's a very good lifestyle.

www.movi.cl

LOUIS-ANTOINE LUYT
LUYT

Louis-Antoine Luyt has a little Indiana Jones about him. Instead of being an obtainer of rare antiquities, Luyt travels around the world sniffing out undiscovered vine treasures. A native Burgundian, he first arrived in Chile in 1998 as a 22-year-old traveler with the idea of exploring South America for three months. It was the start of a passionate relationship with the country and he went on to became the leading advocate for País - the original grapes brought over from Spain by the missionaries.

Luyt ended up staying longer in Chile, finding a job as a dishwasher at a restaurant where he eventually worked his way up to become the wine buyer. While there, he was introduced to South America's only Master of Wine, Hector Vergara, who opened his eyes to the potential of Chilean wine.

Determined that there was something of great potential to unearth, Luyt returned to France in 2002 to learn winemaking, vowing to return to Chile when he was ready. While in France, he became friends with Matthieu Lapierre, son of Beaujolais natural wine pioneer Marcel, and worked five harvests at their estate.

Since his return to Chile, Luyt has helped to bring international attention to the Mission grape. País was first brought over in 1548 by the Spanish friar Francisco de Carabantes. That Chile has some of the world's oldest living vines is due to its natural barriers, Patagonia, the Pacific Ocean, the Andes and the Atacama Desert. This has helped to prevent the arrival of phylloxera, the vine destroying louse that ravaged the vineyards of Europe and the United States.

He has hunted out old, disused or unappreciated vineyards from local growers in the far south of Chile. Luyt's oldest vines have roots dating back from 350 years, or around 1660. He has continued the study

26

of País in other countries, even taking on a País-focused vineyard consulting project in Mexico.

Luyt sources his fruit from 14 small family farmers who dry farm organically and who tend to their vineyards by horse plowing. The winemaking is very traditional and non-interventionist with the grapes being crushed by feet. He vinifies the grapes from each area separately, and the resulting wines are very different, illustrating the importance of terroir to the character of País.

Christopher Barnes: Louis-Antoine, tell us about the region of Bío Bío. It's very far south in Chile.

Louis-Antoine Luyt: It's quite far from the original and traditional Chilean region. We are 500 kilometers south from Santiago. Actually, the southwest region was originally planted in Chile along the Bío Bío River. You also have the Itata River, and we are between both. Maule is another river and region, and the south of Maule and Itata are very close. We buy and we have grapes from these three different river

areas, and the Maule Valley is now the "new old" region. It has been this way for three or four years, and it's a very important region in the wine industry in Chile. It has been planted in continuity with vines for 500 years, mostly since the arrival of the Spanish.

There were three different areas where the Spanish planted vines 500 years ago. These include the north Limari Valley, the Aconcagua Valley in the middle near Valparaíso and Concepción, and the Maule region. In my project, we are looking for the oldest vineyards of these vines. They are mostly planted with Mission grapes.

How old are the vines that you're working with here?

The oldest vineyards where we source our grapes were planted in 1583. They are close to Yumbel. Yumbel is a small town, half an hour from here, and the Mission grapes are mostly between 200 and 400 years old. The other grapes that we picked up are Carignan and Cinsault and are more than 70 years old. They had been introduced in 1979. After 1979, the big earthquake that took place in Chile destroyed all the small cellars. They have since recreated some new cellars and have introduced them to old vineyards with some new grape varieties to produce different wines with more personality in order to be more competitive.

Tell us about the Mission grapes. How did they get to Chile?

When the Spanish conquered America they brought olive trees and wheat.

Wheat. For bread?

Yes. Wheat. The Spanish brought three important things to the region: olive trees, wheat and grapes. They introduced the Mission grapes.

Actually, we saw that there is one Mission grape which is a black one called Negra Criolla. However, they brought five or six different grapes to Chile, some of which we can't find in North America. For the black grapes, it's Listán Prieto, also called Mission or País in Chile. You also have Moscatel de Alejandria, Pedro Ximénez, one that is called Corinth, and Torontel or Torrontés. Another grape for table grapes is Franciscano.

This Mission grape, the País, the black one, you find in Mexico, in Baja California. You find it in New Mexico and in Texas. You find it in California. You find it in Peru, and in many different countries including America. University studies have shown the grape's origins come from Spain, because we find the original grapes in the Canary Islands. Actually I don't know if in Spain they have Listán Prieto, but they have a grape called Listán Negro. Even though prieto and negro mean the same thing, it doesn't mean that it's the same grape. There are studies being done on this, but it's true that the missionaries brought grapes from Spain with them.

It's very interesting. That's what I am surveying now in areas outside of Chile. I'm doing some consulting in Mexico and we find the same grapes and although we have different wines, many things work quite the same.

What are the characteristics of País and are they different in different areas?

Yes. First of all, when I decided to make wine with the País grape, it was about 15 years ago, because someone here in the industry told me there is no way that you can make a good and fine wine with it. My mentality is to go where people say you can't go, so I asked why and if they had ever tried to make a fine wine with País. They told me no. That surprised me because how can you be that sure it's not good if you haven't tried it? I first tried this one place and I realized the wine was very singular. I drove many, many kilometers and I found some small farmers who are still producing wine with these grapes.

From each place, the wines are different. Some things are the same, but many things are different. That means that there is truly identity, or like they say in Burgundy, terroir. Here in Chile, we have an opportunity with one grape which is owned by more than 2,000 people, and when they make their wines, they all have singularity. There are many identities in that. That's what I am doing now by making wines from the same grape, but from different small farmers - from 14 different farmers, from the same grapes, same kind of harvest, and same way of fermentation. That makes true differences.

What are the differences between the 14 different wines from the 14 diverse areas?

Exactly what they state in Burgundy; the terroir, and the last part of the terroir is the winemaker. You have the grapes, you also have the weather conditions, the earth and the grape variety. If you take grapes from Maule, you have wines which are generous in alcohol very early, and you get a large wine with quality. It is mostly the intensity that you can't find because of the age of the vines. The soils are granitic, mainly clay. If you're talking about the Itata region close to the river, you have some terroir that looks like this with granitic soils, but you also have places where you just have sand, and their wines are more floral and the identity is different.

In the Bío Bío region, you have wines that are lighter in alcohol, lighter in color, with more intense spice or herbal notes. There are truly differences. When I am looking in the same region but with different soils, you also have different wines.

Your story is a very interesting one. You're French. You've been in Chile for a long time. You probably told this story a million times, but let's hear it again. How did you end up in Chile?

Well, I was 22 years old. I was in Paris and I was absolutely lost as to what I wanted to do, and I had an experience in 1997 in Australia. I said, well, maybe to find myself, I have to travel. I decided to leave France and my studies and try to find myself in some way in the world. I started seeing the world, Chile, South America. My idea was to cover all of America from south to north and then go back to Australia. Finally, I stayed here because after three months of partying, I decided that I needed to work to continue my journey. I started working in a restaurant and that's where I connected with wine.

We started making a new wine list. It was 1999. I started tasting many wines. I was very impressed and finally a year later, after tasting Chilean wines, I noticed that all the wines were quite similar. After four years in Chile, I decided to go back to France after this guy told me that the Mission grape doesn't work for anything. I went back to France to learn to make wine, to try my opportunity with Chilean Mission grapes.

You learned how to make wine in France, and then you were compelled to come back to Chile?

The idea was to return to France and learn, first of all, if I was able to make wine or if it was just a fantasy. When I went back to France, I discovered that there are many different ways of making wine. In this industry there is industrial, semi-industrial, non-industrial and totally traditional. I prefer the more traditional way. I learned in Burgundy and I worked with some companies in Burgundy, because I wanted to know if I would be able to be a wine producer, not just a winemaker.

Even if after 10 years I started to be more of a winemaker than a wine grower, it's only because I don't have any place in Chilean wine. My favorite job is the process of pruning. The moments of sensitivity, the effort, and when you prune in winter with the freeze, and look back on your line, you can see all the work you've done - some days you have worked a lot, and some days you have not. My evolution brings me more towards the wine process, the winemaking, which I like. But I think it's just a translation to becoming a wine producer, a wine grower, because I think the vine is something really, really sensitive and really, really nice and really, really difficult to grow.

In Chile it's not difficult, in Chile it's easy. You don't have the diseases and infections that are prevalent in Europe. This combination of

events gave me an approach to try to make easy and simple wines with some small and very humble producers. What I've read from wine producers who are my models in Europe, is that wine has to be good anytime you open the bottle. I'd have to say that many times, I have seen bottles that are not good or not as good as I had expected. There are many things in the wine process that you need to manage and to survey, but I think everything starts in the vineyard.

How is the terroir in Bío Bío?

You have many different types of terroir. Here where we are now, it's not an old terroir. It was planted 20 years ago and it's very rich with many organic things. It is something like 12 or 13 percent organic soil. It's very rich, maybe too rich. That's why we try to prune and make some very sensitive wines because there are no problems for the grapes to grow. It's organic culture. Few vines have been planted in this area in these kinds of soils. Traditionally, the Chileans and the Spanish looked for a while to plant in small hills and in infertile soils as they were doing in Europe at this time 500 or 1,000 years ago. These kinds of soils that are rich were for potatoes or crops, anything other than vines.

You have mostly granitic soils, rock and many clays. The soils come from red granite, it means a lot of manganese, a lot of iron in the soils, to yellow clay. As I said before, we also have places on the top of this granitic clay where you have sand, many sands, all volcanic, all from the sea coast, and you have also some pisara which is slate. You have some soils with slate, but it's in the sea coast area. That makes it different than in other places.

When the revolution of wine happened in Chile in the 1990s, the industry planted where it was easy. Now, they need to have more of an identity, so they are going south to source grapes. They pick Mission, they also pick Cinsault. They also have Carignan. Everybody is going back to the roots in a way, looking forward to have more identity in the wines, other than only Cabernet Sauvignon and Chardonnay.

It's very exciting to be here now because in this region, there are many, many different small producers who are able to make good wines, and they are starting to be recognized. That's why we are, I don't know, 40 small producers who are exporting. There was nobody five years ago, perhaps two or three. There is a weight in front of the industry which is a large and big producer with a large plantation. They also are coming here from Casablanca to pick up grapes from this area to make wine because there is a market for this kind of wine. Right now, you have Miguel Torres, Concha y Toro, and many other people who are making wines with Mission grapes. Nobody was doing that five years ago except this vineyard here, Villa Chillán. Nobody was doing it because it was like, "No way." Now, the market has asked for it. There is a change.

What do you see as the challenges for the Chilean wine industry right now?

I don't know. There are many things that we can improve or challenge in Chile. My mission is to tell people, and that the people from Chile understand the Chilean farmers I'm working with. They have to understand that they are able to make good wines and fine wines, that's why I am trying to make the wines as they always have done, taking them to the markets where I'm traveling, and I am lucky because I'm from Europe. I was in Copenhagen, London, Hamburg, Japan and the States, and my customers always look for something simple with identity and with emotion.

I think the most important challenge for the small producers is to understand that their wines are great wines and they have opportunities in the market. At the same time, as the big name companies with all their marketing tools created opportunities, now the markets are open to taste wines that are not branded names; they're looking for wines with emotion and good average prices.

www.louisantoineluyt.cl

ANDREA LEÓN
LAPOSTOLLE

Lapostolle was founded by Alexandra Marnier Lapostolle, great-grand-daughter of the creator of Grand Marnier, and her husband Cyril de Bournet in 1994. Lapostolle's winery in Apalta in the Colchagua Valley is also home to a Relais & Châteaux hotel called The Residence.

Lapostolle owns 370 hectares in three different vineyards and produces a total of 200,000 cases spread over Sauvignon Blanc, Chardonnay, Cabernet Sauvignon, Merlot, Carménère and Syrah.

We speak to Lapostolle winemaker Andrea León about the evolution of Chilean wine, working with famed wine consultant Michel Rolland and the importance of organic farming.

Christopher Barnes: Andrea, tell us about Lapostolle.

Andrea León: Lapostolle came to Chile 20 years ago to make wine here in Colchagua where Alexandra Marnier Lapostolle, the seventh generation of the famous Grand Marnier family, had discovered the amazing potential for producing high-end wines. They began working in Chile, far from their French homeland, and have been here ever since. Now we own three vineyards, in three different appellations, we have two wineries, and we're a mix of Chilean and French, in culture and style of wines.

Michel Rolland was the original wine consultant here and they had an unusual arrangement in which he wasn't allowed to

work for any other winery in Chile. Is that correct?

Well, Alexandra's a very smart lady and I wasn't around at the time, so I just heard the official story, but, yeah, Michel came to Chile and Alexandra asked for exclusivity because she wanted to have him for Lapostolle alone. Also, we have to remember that this was the early '90s so Michel Rolland was not the Michel Rolland we all know today, so he was happy to say yes. Maybe later he wasn't that happy, but, yeah, since then, it's been the only winery he worked for in Chile.

How do you think he has influenced this winery?

Michel's view, simply, is that of the importance of terroir. He comes from Pomerol; he grew up in a vineyard, so I think his view of the vineyard first is very important, and is still very important at Lapostolle.

For the rest, I think, it's the interaction between Alexandra and her own views. The family owns a chateau in Sancerre. She knows about wines. She loves the vineyards when she comes. She spends most of her time tasting grapes or walking the vineyards. Along with Michel's view, that makes Lapostolle's style and core. But I think Alexandra has, I don't know if Michel can see this, as much influence as him in a way. She has her vision and taste. He plays with the raw material we give him to make a reality of Alexandra's vision of the wine she wants to achieve.

Your vineyards are organic. Why did you go down the path of growing organic grapes?

We started the first organic trials back in 2001 and, again, it was

Alexandra's intention to see where that would lead us. Chile is basically very healthy and, in a way, an isolated environment because of our natural barriers, so it seemed a logical path to go that way. We were already moving in that direction and so she said, "Why don't we do some trials?" Then in 2006, we became fully organic and in 2008, we became biodynamic. So, on top of being organic, which was a first step for me, we became biodynamic.

Why? I think there are many reasons. First, she had biodynamics in the back of her head. Her husband, Cyril de Bournet, is related to the Lasserre family in Bourgogne, and that's partly how she was exposed to the biodynamic philosophy. She always had a vision to produce wines related to their origin, and one way to achieve that connection is through biodynamics.

We were not sure it would work so the first step was to be organic, and then the second step was to become biodynamic. Today, we are certified, but it is the will to be good to Mother Nature, in a way, and to ask who lives here and who has to be in the vineyards and eat the grapes.

Also, it's a way to improve quality. But for me, it's more the concept of bringing the terroir more directly into the wine, which is what biodynamics is about.

You started growing on hillsides as well. Tell us about that.

Yes. Many years ago, viticulture traditionally was planted in the flat area, because we had a lot of land. We started to plant on hillsides in the late '90s. We have an estate in Casablanca, which is mostly hillside planted. Here in Apalta, you can see that we started from the bottom and we now have hillside plantations which are more than 200 meters above where we are, which is already 200 meters from the bottom.

Why the hillside? It provides us with a palette for experimentation, for diversity. I wouldn't say the bottom necessarily is better or worse, but it's definitely different and it gives you more elements to achieve balance and complexity in the wines. We believe, as everywhere else in the world, the hillsides are going to be the potential of the wine viticulture for us here.

How have your wines changed over the years?

I think, in part, it is experience. That is something you cannot buy. We are lucky to have very old vines in the vineyard here at the bottom. We have vines that were planted in 1910. I think we have refined many things over the years in terms of vineyard management, harvesting

and how the wines react in the winery, in terms of oak treatment, balance and blending.

I think the wines definitely have changed. We all grow and our palates change, for the better. We are much more complex. We better understand the vineyards. We can separate harvests, separate areas and manage them differently.

Coming back to biodynamics and organic practices, that helps a lot. You need to be very present in the vineyard, and very aware of the differences in order to be successful in your viticulture, and then you'll bring it to the wine. I think if you taste compare older vintages to newer vintages, you can see the difference. it's subtle, but it is there.

How have the changes reflected in the style of the wines?

A good example is our Cuvée Alexandre Chardonnay, which was very much all aged in oak. We planted it in Atalayas, which are vineyards in Casablanca, in the late '90s, and so it was a young vineyard, with oak, and a malolactic style of wine which might be a little bit richer, rounder.

As the vineyard has evolved and grown, and we learned to manage it, we keep more of the acidity, the freshness. Today, it's only half-fermented in oak and half in stainless steel. Half of the oak is new; the other half is used. We don't do any malo.

So, we've found our kind of French style, in a way, but we're not making Burgundy. In Burgundy, you can put new oak, all malo, but here in Chile, it's different and I think we all learned that over the years; it's a classic example. In Apalta with our reds, it's a little bit the same in terms of refinement.

Since the beginning at Lapostolle, we haven't done too much "makeup" in the winery. It's very classic winemaking inspired by France, trying to keep the fruit up front, so I think the mix of barrels probably has changed, but we never filter our wines. We always have done wide fermentation in all our wines from top to bottom. So it's the small adjustments, I think, and with a better understanding in the vineyard that has allowed us to have more purity of the fruit in the bottle later.

Andrea, you worked in France and New Zealand before coming back to Chile. How did you end up working for a French company in Chile?

Well, life has funny ways and I probably had some advantages for the Marnier Lapostolle. I can speak French, which is always good, so I can understand everything and, well, I just clicked with them. The winery here in Apalta was just being built and they needed somebody to be onsite, making the wine here with their vision and I seemed the right person at the right time. I hope they're happy. Well, I think they are because I've been here 10 years now.

You have your own range of experimental wines called The Collection. Tell us about that.

The Collection is some wines we do with Alexandra. It all started with an interest in making more than a single wine. Chile seems very far away sometimes, and we wanted the wine lovers abroad to experience Chile. I have always had an idea to show the terroir effect on small batches of wine with the Shiraz grape variety. This grape adapts well in Chile - very well to cool climate, high altitudes, the inter-mediate valleys. Also, I love Shiraz, so I was happy to experiment.

We did what we call The Collection Shiraz, which is a series of six Shirazes from north to south. Then, after that, we did the Carménère, all from Colchagua so we have three Carménères from the Andes to

the coast, so we showcased the north to south, the east to west. All wines were made with the same style, more fruit-focused, and with very little oak. The idea was to really see the differences.

Right now we are launching Mediterranean varieties, obscure but great varieties that you never see alone. It's really a chance to see a different side of Chile as a collection. It's a group of wines, so you go through them. It's really fun and neat and a great experience.

In terms of the Chilean wine industry, in general, what are some of the challenges that it faces right now?

I think Chile has come a long way for good overall. But, as always, there are new challenges both in the commercial side and in the internal market. It's a great moment for the Chilean wine scene today. I hate the word 'industry' because it doesn't really reflect what wine is. But Chile was born as an industry and is now really moving back to what it truly is, with a generation of both winemakers and wine owners who want to take more risks, to educate more. It's important for the business side, but I think it cannot just be that, so we need to experiment more, which is what is happening.

Also in Chile we took a bit of a challenging route in that we bat for diversity, rather than focus on one grape variety, which is easily related to abroad. So it's perhaps going to take longer, but I think, in the end, it's going to enrich the whole experience of Chile because it's not only wine. It's food, it's people, it's a little bit of what you show in your videos and your books and everything. So we're working, I think, in a good way, but there are still a lot of things to do and improve.

How is it in Chile for female winemakers?

Well, it's challenging, like everywhere in the world, I guess. This is a very demanding job and the harvests are long and intense, and you are away from your family. I think there are a lot of great female winemakers, but it's hard to find a balance right now with family and work, and your passion, because to be a winemaker you need to have a bit of that fire inside you, but it's definitely improving.

Lapostolle Winery
Apalta Km 4
Santa Cruz, Chile
Tel.: +56 72 95 3360
www.lapostolle.com
@LapostolleWine
Watch an interview with Andrea León on YouTube

AURELIO MONTES
MONTES

Two days before interviewing Aurelio Montes at his Apalta estate, I was hanging out sipping wine and eating carne asada at a BBQ in an eastern suburb of Santiago. As the conversation turned to which winemakers we were planning to visit, the interest level rose considerably when Aurelio Montes' name was mentioned. He is regarded as something of a hero in Chile, almost like a national sports star. We tried to think of other countries where a winemaker had achieved such broad popularity and affection and couldn't come up with any.

Part of the appeal of Montes is the that he is self-made. The Chilean wine industry is dominated by three companies, Concho Y Toro (which is now the world's largest wine company), VSPT and Santa Rita, which export 80 percent of the wine from Chile, according to Evan Goldstein's Wines of South America. Montes quit his job at 39 and with five kids, started his winery and built a successful business with no inherited fortune but lots of hard work. He has also gained popularity as Chile's international wine ambassador. Each Montes bottle label says "From Chile with Pride," a statement that has great resonance within the country.

During our visit, Montes took us on a tour of his estate. He is largely responsible for developing Apalta (the word translates to poor soil in the local Indian dialect) and for creating a focus on developing lower yielding, hillside plantings rather than the high density but poor quality fruit of the valley floor. Apalta is a spectacular five-mile-wide amphitheater bordered by the Pangalillo hills located in the Colchagua Valley in central Chile. The Apalta winery was built in 2004 on Feng Shui principles; it is stylish, modern and efficient. Yet this is not a Frank Gehry-starchitect building - function and winemaking are

at the fore. There is a wall in a central location of the winery where they display photos of their importers from around world.

Montes drove us up to a mountaintop ridge overlooking his vineyards in an old pickup truck. It is a majestic spot, even more so as the leaves were changing color. One field of bright fluorescent orange sat adjacent to a field with dramatic yellow hues. We shot our interview and got back into the truck. Montes turned the key and the truck wouldn't start. He called several people on his cell phone to his team back at the winery, but no one was picking up the phone. Awkward moment. We were stuck at the top of a ridge with Chile's most famous winemaker and he was getting a little hot under the collar. It took about five minutes for Montes to reach someone who could walk him through how to start the truck (there was an anti-theft button that needed to be engaged while turning the key).

Aurelio Montes talked to Grape Collective about innovation, dry farming, working with the legendary Ralph Steadman and his path to entrepreneurship.

Christopher Barnes: Aurelio, you were 39 years old with five kids and you decided to start your own business. What was going through your mind at the time?

Aurelio Montes: Well, in general terms, it was a nightmare. It was a very hard decision to make. My five kids were between eight and 15, and I realized what my future without a fixed job and without a payment at the end of the month might be. I couldn't sleep very well for close to a year.

Gladly along the way, while the weeks and months rolled by, I realized we were doing the correct thing because we felt that there was music in the air, that something was going on, something was happening, and everyone was recognizing our job, but it was very, very hard.

Aurelio, it was in 1988 that you first started your business, how did you get it off the ground?

Well, first of all I have to tell you a little story. I wasn't able to do it by myself. I invited three other partners and in the end we became four friends, and partners, each one covering a different area of the business. I always thought four winemakers wouldn't have made it. It was a winemaker, a marketing man, an engineer and a guy who was in charge of finance.

Each of us covered a different part of the whole business. The others had other jobs but I didn't, so I had to start consulting at wineries. Weekends and evenings were enough to start building all of this. Myself, I had to advise and consult different wineries with the same vision as my own, in order to start building all of this.

As things started moving forward and working the way we expected, or even beyond, I consulted less and less. Today, I still have a consulting role for very good friends but it's more of a spiritual thing than anything else.

Chile had traditionally been known for making inexpensive wine that was good for its price, and you were the first to go after the quality segment. How did you come to that conclusion and how did you go about making these better wines that people really embraced?

I studied Oenology at Catholic University. I worked for two years as a winemaker with very well-known, big wineries. Then I got to know the depth, the inside of the industry. I didn't know that while I was studying at the university. I realized Chile was a blessed country, a unique country to produce grapes, and with good grapes you can make good wines.

I saw that we have the coast, we have the northern valleys, we have the southern valleys, we have the Andes, we have this wonderful nourishing of the melting ice that comes to the rivers in the summertime. While making my wines in these different wineries, I realized the range of quality was great. Some of the tanks were amazing quality wines, and they were all blended back to a poor wine at an inexpensive price. My thought was, why don't we start working with the better wines and create another niche in the market, create another category of cheaper wines in the market?

That was my first thought, and then my second thought was, we're established in four different places, four valleys like Maipo, Colchagua, Maule, and so on, and I saw how many different slopes and valleys were there. Putting all these ideas together - I said, "Okay. If we start refreshing the culture, planting in unknown places we will have the potential to grow quality vines and make great wine." That was my belief.

I told all my bosses to go for that. It was a bit dismissed, they were a little bit afraid of the competition with the French, Spanish and Italian wines. I said, "Okay. I will put in the effort. I will try to do it." The market was prepared; the market was ready to receive better wines from Chile at a fairer price.

Making great wine is just part of the equation; you then have to sell the wine. How were you able to succeed in communicating the message that you were making quality

wine here in Chile?

I know, of course. Well, here is where the partnership plays a very important role. One of my partners, Douglas Murray, was an amazingly talented man in marketing. He knew exactly how to approach each of the markets. We had a second positive in that we were the first ones in Chile to come up with this new trend, with the new idea, with this new concept.

As I explained, we surfed the wave all the way along. We saw the wave coming, we jumped on board. There was a beautiful wave, and we surfed it from the very beginning. We were the first ones, we created a curiosity among the importers, distributors, sommeliers and gatekeepers. Basically, they all said, "Well, these guys bring a proposition that seems to be interesting. Let's try the wine."

When they saw the wine was of very good quality, the packaging was good enough, an easy to pronounce Spanish name, Montes, things clicked and worked much faster than we expected. We were very happy with that.

To grow from zero to where you are today, what were some of the key things that happened along the way that were decision points that you look back on and said, "Boy, I'm glad we really did that?"

The key thing that we did was innovation. We were totally different. We did different things that not everyone was doing. We're here in front of these beautiful slopes, no one else before did it. It was expensive to clear out trees, stones, rocks, and slopes and plant. They thought we were crazy, but we did it.

Again, we brought clones from France to refresh our viticulture. The story of Chile as a viticultural paradise is that for the past 150 years we have been reproducing the same cuttings from the vines over and over. There were some endemic viruses and diseases that were already in the plant. I thought, "Okay. Let's get rid of these and let's bring a fresh new concept to viticulture."

We explored valleys. Where we're sitting now, no one else ever thought of planting a vineyard, but we did. Then we went to Marchigüe, a coastal farm, and we were the first ones to arrive there and plant a vineyard. Then we went to Zapallar in the north, no one ever planted a vineyard there and again, we were the first. All of this innovation brought curiosity, openness of the buyers. The whole world would say that "these guys bring an interesting proposition that makes a difference."

Tell us about the winery that you built and the Feng Shui principles behind it.

Again, it's a merit of one of my partners, Douglas Murray. He was very deeply involved in Asian culture, Asian antiques and how they do things in Asia. He was very fond of Feng Shui. When he proposed to bring the concept to the winery, we thought it was a different idea that no one else is doing.

We had a meeting with an expert, a Chilean expert, and we thought the idea was brilliant, it brought happiness to our people. It doesn't mean it brings something magical into the business, but it becomes a nice place to work, where the natural light, the sun, the wood, the metallic things all come together.

The whole idea made a lot of sense and worked with our new concept. Our people work with pride here. Being part of our company in this valley is a matter of pride. When they go to a pub in the afternoon and share a beer with friends and they say, "Well, I work at Montes," it brings me great pride.

Talking about pride, I've spoken with a few Chileans and when your name comes up and the name Montes comes up, people are very proud, proud of what you've accomplished, proud of what the winery has accomplished internationally. One of the things people talk about is that on your labels it says, "From Chile with pride."

That's right.

It's something that really resonates with the people in this country, perhaps you can talk a little bit about it?

Well, within the whole industry, we played an important role, it's a matter of pride. We've changed, let's say, from a poor viticulture of poor quality, in general, in 20 years or so into something very respectful. We are becoming important players in the international arena. We started exporting only three percent of our production in Chile. Today, Chile is a country that exports 70 percent of its production.

Of course, it is a matter of pride. We feel very proud of being part of this very blessed country. It's a beautiful corner of Earth with unbelievable conditions to produce grapes. We have rainy winters, we have sunny springs and summers. It's a place where you want to live, with a very good temperature, and we don't have mold.

We're separated from the rest of the world by very powerful natural barriers like the Andes, the desert in the north and the ocean in the west. All of these make a very unique country and we feel very proud to live in it, so why not say it with pride on the label, from Chile, we're proud of it. I think the whole industry feels the same.

One of the things that is very distinctive about your labels is the illustrations. The illustrator Ralph Steadman has done amazing work, and many people associate him with Hunter S. Thompson and the work that he did with Fear and Loathing in Las Vegas covers. You have his illustrations on your bottles, how did that come about?

Well, it's an old story. We sold a lot of wine to Oddbins in the UK, and Ralph Steadman was the illustrator of Oddbins in his monthly magazine. At some point Oddbins, which was buying a lot of wine from Chile, asked Ralph Steadman to go to Chile, come down here

and personally witness what was going on.

We were asked, as Montes, to take care of him, to look after him. We did, and we became good friends. We moved around the country to the north, to the south. He got involved in the wine industry, we formed a relationship, and when we decided to do some of our wines, especially the Folly, which is a crazy wine, because where it's planted there is ivy, we thought a crazy painter or illustrator would be amazing to make our label.

We asked Ralph Steadman if he would illustrate the label for our wine called Folly, and he said, "Of course. I'd be glad to do that." Every year he changes the label because he paints a lot during his visits to Chile. He's got beautiful landscapes of the north, of our coastal areas, the volcanoes, lakes, Patagonia, so we change the label every year. He even painted a tipsy angel on the back label, a drunk angel, because he thought the wine was so good that even the angel on the label would get drunk.

Aurelio, since your beginnings in 1987, how has your viticulture changed over the years?

One of my views when I started with Montes was to be innovative, and create new things. Although we had good varieties like Merlot, Cabernet Sauvignon, they were overused and over-produced, and there were some endemic diseases, viruses, and so on. I decided to bring fresh clones from France with no viruses, to improve quality and refresh our viticulture, so that was the first step.

Secondly, the trend in Chile was to plant the valley floor with fertile soils and with a lot of water available. The yields were too high and of course the quality wasn't that good. My view, moving around the world, visiting the Rhône valley, the German Rhine, the Mosel, and so on, I realized that we had so many mountains in this country and we could use them.

Having a different type of soil, a poorer granite soil where if you irrigate, or if there is some rainfall, the water drains out very fast, so the plant is always struggling. You control the vigor, you control the canopy expression, you control the yields.

We decided to go uphill. Again, we were thought crazy in this country, planting on the hillside. We had to remove tons of stones, rocks, bushes, and tree trunks. Then we started planting on the slopes, the hillsides, and we realized that the quality was amazing. Lower yields, high concentration, much riper tannins, good expression of flavors and so on. We felt that we were heading in the right direction. That was the second point to address.

Then the third one was that we were established in two or three different valleys in Chile, and we thought there were so many other alternatives unexplored, undiscovered. We started to move to new spots, the coast, hillsides, some valleys totally poor in terms of agriculture that people thought unsuitable. We proved that the vines did grow, and did grow very well there. All of these elements created a kind of little revolution in viticulture.

Tell us about dry farming, it's something that doesn't really happen in this part of Chile.

Well, dry farming is something that is used worldwide. All of Europe uses it because Europe has a lot of rainfall during the summertime. You have to realize that Chile, because of its geographical position, because of the Humboldt Current and the presence of the Pacific Ocean, it doesn't rain in spring or summer.

Going to dry farming is quite risky, but global warming is hitting Chile as well, we're no exception. The rainfall comes less and less, it's more scarce. My thought was I want to know hell before I go there forever, I wanted to know how to react if someday there's no longer any rain. We stopped irrigating a small part of the vineyard, with the risk of killing the vineyard, but I was determined to do it.

We were very impressed and astonished to discover that the vines didn't die. They could react to drought, they could adapt themselves to the drought, they dug deeper into the subsoil, and of course we helped with some wood covers, shortening the canopy. We found that by lowering the yields we could live without irrigation.

From the year 2012 onward in our Montes Alpha range, we decided to go to dry farming. We are the only winery doing this in these valleys. If you go to the southern valleys where there is some rain in summer, they normally do dry farming, but in these valleys it's quite unique.

How much water are you saving?

We're saving a lot of water. Just to give you a couple of figures, we went from 4,000 cubic meters down to 1,000 cubic meters per hectare. The amount of water we are saving is exactly the needs of 20,000 people per year. We are in a very sustainable situation using less water, less energy, and saving water for human needs.

How does dry farming impact the quality of the wine that you're making?

To be very honest, when I started the project of dry farming I was trying to save water without affecting much of the quality, but what we found after five years, we have been doing a lot of research, is that we saved a lot of water, and we improved the quality, too. It was something that I didn't expect.

The yields went from 10 tons to the hectare down to five or six, nearly half. The cluster size from 150 grams went to 90, just a smaller cluster, but much more concentrated, the tannins are riper, with a high concentration of flavors and color. Phenolics, everything is much better. As an extra bonus, we got a better quality out of this dry farming.

In terms of the Chilean wine industry, what are some of the challenges that it faces?

Technologically speaking, we are up to the level of any wine producing country, even the most modern, such as Napa Valley in California.

We have very fresh viticulture; we have wonderful tools to work with in oenology. I would say the biggest challenge the industry is facing today is the market.

We have to prove to the world that we are able to produce amazing quality wine. We have to keep working, producing high quality wines, we shouldn't lose focus. The Chilean wine industry must always be aiming towards quality, to over-deliver, and teach people that Chile is a good alternative in terms of wine.

How do you see the future of Chilean wine? People have talked about Carménère being the grape of Chile. Is Cabernet Sauvignon the grape of Chile? Will Chile be a country like Argentina that puts itself behind one varietal, or are you going to focus on many varietals?

I would say that the name of Chile is diversity. We have wonderful natural conditions. Today we have more than 16 different valleys. We have proven that many different varieties work pretty well in all of these alternatives. We're producing amazing wines in the coastal region with the cold climate, like amazing Sauvignon Blancs, Pinot Noirs, Chardonnays and Rieslings.

We're producing amazing wines in the Central Valley, the best reds, Syrahs, Cabernets, Carménère of course. We're starting to explore the foothills of the Andes. We are not standing behind any specific variety. I would say that the most attractive part of Chile is its diversity, and quality across the board.

Talk about the terroir of Apalta. This is a very unique spot that we're in right now. Is the climate and the soil unique in this part of Chile?

Well, we are within Colchagua Valley and Apalta is a little spot within this big valley. We have very unique conditions here. We have a beautiful range of mountains behind us facing the north. We have the Tinguiririca River in the south that creates a microclimate here.

The valley being slightly warm, the fact that we are facing south, the south side is the cold side in Chile. It's cooler, so we have a late sunrise and an early sunset. In addition to that, the temperatures are not that high, we have a very specific granitic soil, a decomposed granitic soil with a certain component of limestone and clay that make the soil fantastic to grow most of the red varieties.

The Syrahs, Carménère, Petit Verdot, Cabernet Franc are the most amazing varieties that I've produced on the slope. As you move down to the valley floor, the Cabernet Sauvignon becomes an amazing variety that has adapted very well too.

Chile has always been known for inexpensive wines, how does Chile promote what you're doing here? How do you get the word out to the rest of the world that you're producing quality wines?

Well, there are many ways of course. I think that I'm becoming a little bit political. I think that the government should realize that investing in the image of Chile is very important. We have a lot of priorities in our country, but investing in image is so important.

People should know about Chile, and should know about Chile beyond wine. They should know about its beauty, the natural beauty that we have in our landscape. They should know a little bit about our food, we have amazing local food, and they should know about our people. The Chileans are amazingly friendly people. Although, lots of foreigners are coming, we should make an extra effort to bring more people, especially from the wine business.

Of course to realize, to witness all that we're seeing today, this beautiful landscape, the granitic soils, the commitment to quality wine, it will all take time. It doesn't happen overnight. It will take years and maybe a couple of generations, but we're heading in the right direction and we shouldn't stop.

Aurelio, you created a winery in Mendoza, Argentina. You also started making wine in Napa. What made you decide to go outside of Chile to make wine?

At some point, after 15 years at Montes, we had already established a brand in the marketplace that was quite unique. We felt that we were quite consolidated here, but we still had energy to burn. We wanted to do something else. Chile was covered, so the natural next step was to move to Argentina, which is next door.

By plane, it takes half an hour to get there, or four hours by car. We have a similar culture with the people there, with the winemakers, with viticulture. That was our first step and we don't regret it. Things have been going very well there. We established a very nice winery, we own land and we own our own winery.

My son Aurelio Jr. is in charge of that operation and he lives in Mendoza, Argentina. It's been a wonderful experience. We found friendly people, very focused on quality as well. We have a second brand that is quite known, not as well-known as Montes, but it's quite known, it's called Kaiken, the name of this wild bird that flies back and forth across the Andes, just as we did. We did it and we're happy. It's been a success in my opinion.

Then four or five years after we started in Argentina, I felt that we still needed to do something else to prove to the world, and prove to ourselves, that we could produce wine anywhere. Napa is a cathedral to New World quality wines, and we wanted to be side by side with the Mondavis, with Francis Ford Coppola, with all these trendy names, the Screaming Eagles and the Harlans and so on, and prove to the world that we could produce good wines there, and we did it.

In the year 2006 we started with a very small operation. We process our wines in our winery in Carneros, in the southern part of the Napa Valley. We are already in the market with very good write-ups, and very good comments on the wines. It will always be a small operation, but it's a little bit like the cherry on top.

Apalta Winery and Vineyards Viña Montes
Parcela 15 - Millahue de Apalta
Santa Cruz, Chile
Tel.: (56-72) 2817815 Ext. 108-101
Email: lafinca@monteswines.com
www.monteswines.com

ENZO PANDOLFI
PANDOLFI PRICE

Pandolfi Price started in 2002 with Santa Ines, a single vineyard on the banks of Larqui in Itata, in Southern Chile. Their first wine was a dry Chardonnay, planted in 1992.

Pandolfi Price has received acclaim for their Chardonnay - not a grape traditionally associated with Chile. They were featured in our rising stars of Chile column and are represented in the UK by the well-respected retailer Berry Bros. & Rudd.

We speak to Enzo Pandolfi about the Itata region and the challenges of being a small, quality-focused winemaker in Chile.

Christopher Barnes: Enzo, tell us how you got into the wine business.

Enzo Pandolfi: Actually, we got there by, I think destiny, chance, a combination of a lot of things. My parents were, and still are, very into farming and a few years ago they had a chance to invest in a farm. They got a farm that happened to have some vineyards on it. Bam! Eight years later, we're making wine and we're really fascinated with it. We've learned a lot and we still have a lot to learn, but I think the road we're taking is very interesting and we're very fond of it.

You started growing grapes. How did you make the transition from producing and selling grapes to making your own wine?

Well, we started with a planted vineyard and we knew nothing. So we began to learn and understand how everything works by consulting with lots of advisers who were telling us what to do. At one point, we realized okay, this gets simpler, it gets easier. We then began to

understand the great thing about vineyards is that the grapes capture the surroundings. So since we're so fond of Sta. Ines, which is our farm, our vineyard, we wanted to create a product that reflected it. No matter how good or bad it was, we just wanted to see where it would go and what we could get. Maybe it was destiny, but we happened to bump into a great winemaker who does this really well, which is respecting the terroir, and preserving the terroir in the wine that he makes. That's the point where we're at right now, just letting the terroir express itself and letting the wine show what the terroir has to offer.

Enzo, your wines are from Itata. What is the terroir of Itata, and what is the terroir of your farm?

Itata is further south than the common Chilean valleys, or the well-known ones, and that gives you a cooler climate. It also has very old soils. You have Cordillera La Costa and the Andes, the Central

Valley and the ocean. Many of the soils we have here are dominated by volcanoes. We have the Chillán volcano quite near us, and the Cordillera La Costa, which are old granites. So we have a combination of terroirs here with cool climate, great acidity, volcanic soils expressed by clay and volcanic ash layers, and very old granites from Cordillera La Costa. So you combine all that and you get really old stuff. It's very interesting what we have in here.

You specialize in Chardonnay at the moment, is that correct?

Yes.

Enzo, in a very short period of time, you've been able to produce wines at a very high level. How did you go from zero to where you are right now?

First of all, I think we were where we needed to be at the right moment. We met the right people, we learned from people who respected the terroir and we started fresh from there. We didn't get any advice from anywhere else. I think that combination and the conviction that Sta. Ines was a great place to grow grapes got us the results we're getting right now. Again, a bit of chance, a bit of luck and timing, and it all came together.

How do you describe the Chardonnays that you're making?

Real, authentic, terroir-driven, Itata, Sta. Ines, intense. I think they're powerful with a huge personality. I don't want to get more technical because it's Itata, that's it.

Your wines are being sold by Berry Bros. & Rudd, which I think is a great testament to their quality. Berry Bros. is one of the oldest wine merchants in the world. They represent the best wines in the world and they selected your wines. You must have been very pleased when you were able to strike that deal.

Yes, actually. When we got together, I'm almost a nobody in the wine business, nobody knows me. I sat on the other side of the table with one of the buyers of Berry. We started tasting and I watched his face when he was trying it. He was very impressed because he wasn't expecting that. He said this doesn't even look like Chile. And it's not Chile, it's Itata. It's Sta. Ines again. It's a great energy punch for us, it's another breath to keep going. It's an assurance that what we're doing, even though it takes a long time, is the right way to go. That gives us tranquility and patience to wait for what's coming.

You've now developed a second area of vineyards focused on red grapes. Can you tell us a bit about that?

58

Well, we had another piece of the farm, of the vineyard, that wasn't being used. It was wasted land. Knowing little because once again we're not farmers, we started thinking, okay, we've been learning from the vineyards for eight years now, why don't we see if we can get red in the vineyards up here too? So we contacted a very well-known professional, Pedro Parra, who happens to live right near us. He really knows his stuff. He's a terroir expert, one of only a few in the world, and so we contacted him. He did a terroir evaluation of our soils, our land, and our climate and reached the conclusion that what we had was very promising. So we went for cool-climate reds like Pinot Noir and Syrah, and we added a bit of Sauvignon Blanc to complement the Chardonnay we're making. Pedro assigned us a very neat plantation with different expositions, with different soils, with very small plots, different clones, so we'll get a very big palette of colors in order to play with our wines and get extremely good wines at the end.

What would you say are the challenges facing the Chilean wine industry at the moment?

I think that it's getting people to understand that Chile is not only cheap and good, but it's also very good, and with reasonable value. There's more to tell than just the big industries, and Chile is known right now because of the big industries - Concha Y Toro, Montes, Errázuriz, which are the very big ones, but there's a whole new movement right now, the very small projects, terroir-driven projects, which are showing a new face of Chile, which are showing maybe the real Chile, the land, the soil, the climate we have.

How do you see the future of Chilean wine?

I think it's quite promising. It's shifting its boundaries towards south and north, and towards the coast. It's a bit cooler because of the Central Valley up north, it's quite hot right now, or it's shifting from the center to the sides, I think. Up, down, left, and right. Andes, ocean, north, and south. I think what we're going to see in the next few years is quite interesting and quite exciting wines.

www.pandolfiprice.cl

GRANT PHELPS
CASAS DEL BOSQUE

He's from New Zealand, is a professional DJ on the side and has made wine in South America for 15 years. Grant Phelps may be Chile's most unusual winemaker.

Prior to settling in Chile, Phelps worked as a flying winemaker in Australia, Argentina, California, Hungary, New Zealand and Oregon. He is currently head winemaker at Casas del Bosque in the cool-climate Casablanca Valley region, which hugs Chile's Pacific coast.

We talk to Phelps about being a winemaker/DJ, his wine journey and the potential of Chilean wine.

Christopher Barnes: Is Chile making good Pinot Noir right now?

Grant Phelps: I think it is. It's changed compared to 20 years ago when I tasted my first Chilean Pinot. My first experience with Chilean wine was in 1996 in London, at the annual tasting the industry puts on there, and the first things I tasted were all the Pinots in the room. The Pinots back then were all over-extracted, lousy oak, you could tell they were over-cropped and coming from areas that were way too hot. That was the reality back in the mid '90s. What got planted was in the Central Valley between the coastal mountain range and the Andes.

You had a lot of Pinot that was brought into Chile to spike the wine production to the high-yielding variety, high-yielding selections. Many planted the pergola or the head system, over-cropped, you're talking

10, 12 tons per acre, probably flood irrigated and obviously the area is way too hot for Pinot anyway. Winemakers back then hadn't come into contact with the real Pinot Noir. Back in the mid '90s Chilean winemakers really hadn't traveled and made wine in other regions before coming back to Chile to work, to set up camp. What you saw were these Pinots that were just overworked in the winery, over-extracted, very stringent.

Also the oak selection generally was very sketchy chips and staves and not great wood. Bearing in mind that these were Pinots made at that time for the English supermarket trade, so we're talking very low-end in terms of cost, probably six to eight dollars retail on the shelves. Not expensive wines. Then of course what happened in Chile was new cool-climate regions like Casablanca where we are right now. This was the first cool-climate region. It was just starting to happen in the mid '90s, and of course with any new region there is a learning curve. You have to remember at this point that Chile had been making wine for about 500 years.

In the mid '90s, Chileans were clear on how to work with hot-climate varieties in the hot areas of Chile, but the cool-climate thing was completely new, and I think they were a bit lost. It took them a few years, but I think probably, in my mind around 2005 onwards, Chile started making serious world class Pinot Noir. Casablanca, Leyda, also now coastal valleys and coastal parts of valleys, such as Elqui and Limari further up north, and even now in Atacama there are some interesting Pinots coming out of there. And we're talking way extreme north desert, so there is serious Pinot being made in Chile. Also what's happened down south in the past probably three to five years since that natural winemaking thing started to happen. There are some French guys down there making some interesting Pinot Noirs. I wouldn't say they're classics, sort of textbook Pinot. It's not necessarily what I love, but it's definitely a counterpoint to the more polished, fresher, cooler-climate versions being made right now.

You said "world class," how would you define them in terms of their characteristics relative to some of the areas people think about, when they think about Pinot Noir?

I wouldn't go Burgundy. I think it's a big mistake to compare a New World region to Burgundy. I think Oregon has learned from that, so did central Otago, New Zealand, 10 or 15 years ago when these regions were getting started, or 20 in the case of Oregon at least. A lot of people were drawing parallels with Burgundy. I don't hear that so much anymore. I think everyone is clear they're not trying to make Burgundy, and I'd say the same thing about Chile. Chile 15 years ago, probably, was talking a lot about Burgundy.

So what are the characteristics of Chilean Pinot Noir?

I think if I were to compare Chile elsewhere, it definitely wouldn't be Burgundy. Depending on where you are and the style of the winemaker, I think some of our wines are a little bit more comparable to central Otago, because there are good savory notes in our Pinot Noir, especially in this part of Casablanca. Here we're on the very coastal edge of Casablanca. We're talking hillsides planted on 120 million-year-old granite with red volcanic clay on top. I get a little savory note with my saline character coming through on the Pinot Noirs, which reminds me a lot of central Otago. In general, if you look at cool-climate Chile and you compare it to somewhere else, I think we're probably more Californian in style. I would say more of Russian River, Sonoma and on the coast.

Not so much Oregon. Oregon tends to be, especially in the heart, very big and very rich Pinot Noirs. I don't think we're quite at that extreme level of voluptuousness. I think we're a little bit more fresh, a little bit more elegant, and it depends a little bit on the vintage in the area. Places such as Casablanca and Leyda are quite cool. We are a bit cooler even than the Russian River, so I think we tend to edge more towards a little bit more elegance.

I'm searching for my Humphrey Bogart quote but tell us about Casablanca.

Casablanca is not in Morocco! Not this Casablanca. Casablanca was the first cool-climate region developed in Chile. The very first experimental plantations happened in about 1983, and the commercial production of grapes didn't begin until about '89. So the first wines really hit the shelves about 1990, '91. The wines didn't get exported until probably about '93 to '95, something like that. In terms of existing, at least internationally, Casablanca is only about 20 years old. It is interesting that Chile has been making wine for 500 years, but it has only been 20 years that we've been working in cooler, more coastal regions. The rest of the world has a strong relationship between north and south in the amount of heat, but that's not the case in Chile.

Chile is the longest, skinniest country in the world, and wine is grown now in an incredibly large part of that north to south stretch. But you can be south and up against the Andes, and it can be relatively hot. It might be quite a short growing season, but during the growing season you get very high temperatures. You can get well above 90 degrees everyday. But you can be way further north and close to the coast and it's super cold, like Casablanca. We're due west of Santiago which is pretty much in the dead middle - dead center of the country. Santiago is very hot, but coming up the coast we have this very good cold current of water called the Humboldt Current. It originates in Antarctica, and runs all the way back to Chile, Peru, hits Ecuador and swims out towards the Galapagos where it finishes up. Here, it's very, very cold. It runs between 14 and 16 degrees Celsius - winter to summer, so you're probably talking ... I'm not very good with my Fahrenheit conversion, probably, talking 45 to 50. Something like that. As a temperature shift, it's cold. To put it in terms you can understand - you can cut glass with your nipples I think in about two minutes of getting into the water.

Okay.

It's pretty damn cold. So the effect that it has is essentially where we are in Casablanca, between Casablanca and Maipo (which is on the other side of the coastal mountain range), there is a strong series of mountains. When the air heats up in the morning and replaces that hot mass which is rising, it can't get to the Santiago, Maipo way

because it's blocked by the mountains. It has to come from the ocean, and that air that comes in is very, very cold, and it draws in fog as well. We typically get fog rolling in the late afternoon, and it blankets the valley until mid-morning the next day, then the sun obviously burns it off. We get hot sunny weather and then the fog rolls in again, and that's about the classic pattern.

We always get a very cold wind coming in off the ocean that generally precedes the fog. It has a very strong cooling effect, and that's why this valley is so cold. We rack up this side of the valley where we are close to the ocean, about 750 growing degree days Celsius in your average season. On the other side of the valley over towards Santiago and 10 miles in a straight line there are about 950 growing degree days, so it's about 20 percent hotter just in that 10 mile east-to-west shift from where we are now west-to-east shift, so it's a big difference. 950 is about the same as Sonoma, 750 is about the same as Champagne.

Here it's very, very cold, but we get stuff ripe here that wouldn't ripen in Champagne simply because it's sunny, generally, whereas in Champagne during the growing season you have a lot of cloudy days.

Grant, coming from New Zealand, the grape everyone associates with New Zealand is Sauvignon Blanc and you make Sauvignon Blanc. How has the experience of making Sauvignon Blanc in New Zealand interacted with the terroir of Chile?

64

Well, I would say it kind of hasn't, to be honest. Growing up a New Zealander, obviously Sauvignon Blanc was the first wine I discovered. It was the epiphany moment for me, and it's what got me into wine and so for that I'm eternally grateful. But by the same token as most New Zealand winemakers, if they're being frank with you, will tell you the one thing no one wants to make anymore as a New Zealander winemaker is Sauvignon Blanc. Generally the wines are obviously very characteristic, people can recognize them. In a blind tasting, it's obvious what's from New Zealand, but by the same token that makes the wines a little bit the same. And that really in-your-face, cat pee, gooseberry bush, that thing is quite inherently food incompatible to me and that's something I kind of rebel against as a winemaker.

Obviously when I was working in New Zealand I had to make a lot of Sauvignon Blanc. A necessary evil if you like. I do every now and then drink a bottle of Sauvignon Blanc from New Zealand. I don't completely hate the stuff, or anything like that. I like to drink wine with food generally, and I think the Marlborough style wines are very in your face aromatically, and then in the mouth they tend not to really be there much. The wines are fresh, but they're very simple and they're quite diluted as well, for the most part. It's just that sensation, the acidity, but with food I don't really like to drink New Zealand Sauvignon Blanc. There are maybe three exceptions, three wines I think are made in a more complex style in New Zealand with a bit of oak, a bit of malolactic fermentation, maybe trying to be more of a gastronomic style.

It can be done, it's just not what people are trying to make in New Zealand, and you know, that's because the consumers who buy New Zealand Sauvignon Blanc want that in-your-face, asparagus, gooseberry, cat pee thing. What I really liked about making Sauvignon Blanc when I came to Chile ... I made Sauvignon Blanc in a bunch of other places first. I worked within the States, Australia, France and Hungary even, but I came to Chile and what I really liked about the Sauvignon I found here was that it's very, very citrus driven. It's not green and herbaceous and vegetal. It's much more citrus, and if you want to make a Sauvignon Blanc here with nice texture, mouthfeel, you can. It works well with that style.

The other thing is, in Chile, the Sauvignon is grown in the cool areas of Chile, like Leyda and Casablanca, which have great natural acidity and great natural balance. In New Zealand, generally, the wines are picked with low sugars and very high acidities and you need to, as a winemaker, de-acidify and chaptalize and everything else to make the wine just a bit more balanced. In Chile that's not the case. I literally don't have to manipulate these wines at all in terms of alcohol or acidity. What you get is what you see. What we do which is very, very different here, and once again, going back to that thing about trying to make a wine with Sauvignon that is more food compatible. We're picking 100 percent at night. We're the last people in the valley, we're probably the last people in Chile, to pick their Sauvignon Blanc.

We start picking - in an average a year - after the 20th of March, so it's a good month after they start picking Sauvignon Blanc on the other side of the valley. That's only 10 miles away, but there's a huge difference. We are picking a full month after they are, and we're picking 100 percent at night. The reason being: the temperatures are much lower at night here - obviously, but here we get a huge shift in temperature. At the end of March we'll be getting up into the mid 20s during the day - so probably mid 80s in Fahrenheit - but at night we will be dropping down below 10 degrees Celsius - so low to mid 40s maybe at the start of evening.

We start picking at 11:00 p.m. and we pick through until 6:00 a.m. The grapes will come in naturally at seven, eight degrees at the start of evening, and by the time we finish picking at 6:00 in the morning, they're down to about four degrees Celsius. The grapes are naturally cold and then we're going to crush pad very differently - we are only just stemming. We de-stem, we don't go to press. We actually have a tank so we do full skin contact. We go into tank via a heat exchanger, so we're chilling the grapes down to between minus one and minus three degrees Celsius. Fahrenheit no idea - 25 to 30 degrees, something like that. The grapes go into stands in the steel tanks, extremely cold, and we're just soaking on skins and we're doing extended maceration. Minimum seven days up to 11 days on skins before we drain and press. That's different. I'm sure someone else somewhere in the world does something similar but I certainly haven't heard about it. Definitely no one in Chile is doing 100 percent skin contact on their whites, and definitely not for seven to 11 days, that's a pretty long time.

Why do we soak on skins? The reasons are twofold. First off, this vineyard has very unique soils. We have granites which were formed via cementation under the Pacific Ocean 120 million years ago during the Cretaceous Period, and then uplifted via plate tectonic movement. Casablanca's unique in Chile in that it's the only wine producing valley with no river. So why is there no river? Because the coastal mountain range at the head of the valley is completely intact.

The glaciers in the last ice age that originated in the Andes never managed to breach and make it all the way up to the ocean, as they did in all the wine producing valleys in Chile. Everywhere there is a valley that runs pretty much east to west in the Andes up to the ocean and first the glaciers curved that valley out, and then later on as the glaciers receded it was followed by rivers. With the rivers you get the alluvial action of stones and new material coming down from the Andes and being deposited on the surface of the original soils, because there is no river here and there was never any glacier and the coastal mountain ranges are intact. We've never had any movement of any material in the valley.

The soils are about 120 million-year-old granites, which are right on the surface now. They're actually below only about 30 centimeters of top soil, so the roots are actually right within the granite layer. That has a very strong impact on the flavor profile of the wines, but it only has a strong impact if you do skin contact. If you press the grapes straight away, all the flavors in the skins - there is essentially no time for the juice to pick up that flavor.

We're trying to pick up that flavor and just, if you like, turn the volume up on the amplifier. Just soak the juice extremely, extremely cold with the skins for those seven days to extract that flavor.

The reason the temperature is important is twofold. First, we don't want the juice to start fermenting on the skins. Obviously the grapes come in with native yeast from the vineyards, so you have to be very careful that the fermentation doesn't kick off in the skins, or you wind up with a wine that smells remarkably like baby sick. Not so attractive.

Secondly at this point the seeds are still in there so the very low temperatures are important because I just want to check the skins, not the seeds. If you're getting above zero degrees, up close to 10 degrees maybe 45 degrees Fahrenheit you're going to be extracting preferentially from the seeds, which leaves tannins, and you're talking about bitter phenolic compounds.

Tannins or phenols that come from the skins are totally different in terms of the part of the mouth they attack, in terms of the sensation they generate. I don't think you can see it if you taste the wine. If you get it into your mouth and you chew it you'll get the sensation that the ferment hits the walls of your mouth and the tongue, and it gives you a slight puckering sensation. It's almost like you're biting into the rind of a grapefruit or something like that. It's phenolic, if you like, bitter, but it's a very agreeable bitter sensation. That's what I'm trying to achieve with this wine - just that real puckering sensation.

How long did it take you to come up with this methodology of creating Sauvignon Blanc? You inherited a way of doing things, and then clearly you've changed things fairly radically.

Well, I started playing around with skin contact my first year in Chile 15 years ago. I was working further south in a hotter region and I was dealing with Sauvignon Blanc. It's a place where Sauvignon Blanc shouldn't be growing because it's way too hot, but I had a little Sauvignon and I had to make Sauvignon Blanc, so obviously I went into it basically picking on flavor. In hotter areas Sauvignon Blanc will hit its flavor peak much earlier than it does here in Casablanca. Here most of our Sauvignon is pushing 14 degrees alcohol, and that's just because the sugars do their own thing and the flavors accumulate differently. It's all about picking quality flavor for me. In Colchagua where I was before, Sauvignon would be hitting it's flavor peak at about 11 degrees alcohol, not at 14. We would be picking much earlier, but you would be out there and you'd taste the grapes everyday.

Sauvignon changes very rapidly in terms of flavor, so you do have to be there everyday and trying to hit that sweet spot. In the vineyard I would taste the grapes until I'd get to the point where I felt the flavors were right on and we would pick the grapes, but then the grapes would come in. Once you're in the night harvest the grapes are cold, and then into the press, and pressing, I would taste the juice coming out of the press, and I would be thinking, "This just doesn't taste like it did in the vineyard, and I was out there this morning." I started to think back in New Zealand we don't make skin contact, not deliberately, but everything's machine picked in New Zealand, and it goes into the back of dump trucks essentially.

When I was with Villa Maria back in the mid '90s, all the best Sauvignon would go up to the Auckland winery to be processed, but it was all coming from Marlborough. Obviously it was machine picked at night, and into the back of dump trucks in the morning. In the morning it went on the ferry. It would travel from South Island over to the North Island, then it would take about eight hours to get to the winery. We were normally processing it 24 hours or even longer after the grapes were picked, and during all this time it was sloshing about in the back of the truck. I started to think it's not intentional skin contact, but it's still contact, so I started playing around with it. It worked really, really well. I started playing around for six hours, and then it went to 12 hours, and then 24.

I came to Casas del Bosque six years ago, and I was already convinced that skin contact was the way to go. Plus, here we have great soils, which wasn't the case in Colchagua. In Colchagua, I wanted to pick up the phenolic compounds from the skins to give the wines a bit more texture, but here is where I entered the secondary consideration of getting the flavor from the vineyard into the wine, so I went more extreme. Plus, because harvest is so much later here since the grapes ripen later, and because it's a cooler area, that gave me the possibility to get the grapes into tanks so much colder than I could in Colchagua. I've just extended their time.

I started off three days six years ago, and then I went to four, and now I've gone up towards as much as 11. For me it works. It gives you an amazing sensation in the mouth, plus that vineyard character comes through so much stronger. I think you can see here in this glass. You get this real sensation of silver white pepper and ginger. The salinity comes through clearly and that's coming from the soils. It's only there because we skin contacted the grapes.

Grant, you used to be a DJ. How did you get into DJ'ing and then winemaking?

I've always loved music. I grew up listening to lots of music, and I bought my first record by saving my pocket money - I think we all did back then - to buy records. I just started DJ'ing with a couple of friends. We pooled our money to buy a set of decks and started DJ'ing parties and setting up parties on our own. I got into winemaking because I was already traveling a lot with the winemaking thing. The International DJ thing worked in pretty well sometimes. If I happened to be somewhere selling wine, every now and then I got offered a DJ'ing spot at a party, or a rave, or what have you.

I don't do it so much anymore, because I'm pretty busy making wine, but last year I DJ'd a party in Toronto. A couple of years ago I did Bogotá. So I still do an international gig every now and then, but it's definitely not at the forefront.

What's the most fun you ever had doing a DJ event?

There's been so many of them, and some of the experiences are very, very random. Probably one of the weirdest gigs I ever did related to wine was for our importer in Colombia. He owns a bunch of health spas and restaurants. I was up there a couple years ago doing a winemaker dinner at one of his restaurants, and as I arrived he said, "Oh, Grant, I thought I'd set up a party at the spa seeing as you're here, and I thought you could DJ and a buddy of mine is a local musician, he's going to accompany you." I thought, "That's weird. I don't usually have someone accompanying me when I'm DJ'ing." I turned up at the party, fortunately I had some music with me on MP3, and I was introduced to this guy, Carlo Vives, who is a really famous musician in Colombia. I didn't know it at the time. I had no idea who he was. He was there accompanied by his wife, who was the former Miss Colombia. She was up there in the DJ booth with us, and basically I was mixing records, and mixing MP3, and he was sitting there with his bongo drums playing along, so it was pretty surreal.

How did you get into making wine?

To be honest, I was doing my first degree in zoology at university in New Zealand, and I started working in bars to pay my way through university, as you do. Night jobs. I started pouring wine across the bar, and people would ask about the wine and I just became interested and started reading about wine, literally in my spare time. I started drinking a bit of wine and going to tastings. It was something I found really interesting. One night I was literally pouring a glass of Pinot for this guy. He said, "Grant, tell me about this Pinot," and I replied, "Santa Lina Pinot Noir, first New Zealand wine to get a gold medal in London, blah, blah, blah," and he goes, "Man, you know a lot about wine. You should study to be a winemaker." I think I was 19 or 20 years old at the time, and I said, "Surely that's not a job." He said, "Yeah, there's a university nearby with a wine program. You should check it out." I went the next day and literally enrolled. It was the last day of enrollment, and I thought, "Hey, why not?"

Then you were a flying winemaker for a while.

Worked as a flying winemaker, yeah, in the mid to late '90s. I worked for three different English companies making wine for them in different parts of the world. With those guys I wound up working in California, Hungary, France, and Argentina, and eventually in Chile.

You came to Chile and then you stayed. How long have you been here?

I've been here for 15 years now.

That's a long time.

There are more harvests in Chile than anywhere else in the world.

Even more than in New Zealand, so yeah this is officially home.

What was it about Chile that grabbed you?

I think it was the eighth country that I arrived in to make wine. Obviously you work in different regions, and you take different winemaking experiences from each region, but I think what really surprised me the most about coming to Chile, and I thought I'd seen it all, was just the amount of old vineyards. There's no phylloxera in Chile. I found myself making entry level supermarket wines for the UK market from 100- or 120-year-old Cabernet vineyards. Unirrigated. These are spectacular vineyards, and it's just a piece of history, and you don't see that anywhere else in the world. A 120-year-old old Cab vineyard in California would be a rarity, and it would be incredibly expensive. It wouldn't be going into a five or six pound bottle of wine. Whereas in Chile, that kind of thing is still reasonably widespread. For our entry level Cabernet here, I buy a big chunk of the grapes for that blend from a vineyard planted in the year 1900.

A lot of what I love about being a winemaker is the tradition and the history. Countless other winemakers before me have fermented the same grapes and made their versions of this vineyard that translate into the bottle. To be able to do that now, to be able to make wine from a vineyard planted before even my grandfather was born, that's still pretty cool.

Tell us about Casas del Bosque.

Casas del Bosque is a family winery - owned by the Cuneo family. They started the project originally as just a vineyard, producing and selling grapes. That was in the year 1993 when Casablanca was just getting started, and they were the first to plant on this side of the valley. This is the most seaward side, therefore the most frost-prone, the coldest part of the valley. At that time no one was really sure whether it was economically viable to produce grapes here, so they were the first to plant a vineyard here. It started off just as a vineyard, and then in 2000 they started making their own wine on a very small scale. Eventually the winery was built, and now we've transmogrified, if you like, into a 130,000 case-a-year winery. We're still relatively small by Chilean standards, but no longer a hobby winery, so to speak.

What do you see as the challenges Chile faces as a wine country?

I've been here 15 years, so I've seen quite a few changes already. I think the big challenge for Chile has been, and still is, that it's dominated by massive wineries. Massive wineries, as anywhere in the world, as in California or Australia for example, tend to make pretty bland, pretty uninteresting wines. About 80 percent of what Chile is producing is still coming from three players in the Chilean market: Concha Y Toro, San Pedro and Santa Rita. I think the problem is that if you are a wine consumer tasting Chilean wines, chances are you're going to taste one of the wines from the three big guys, and I don't know if you're going to be unimpressed. I think the wines they make are generally really good value for the money. Nice wines, but you're not going to be blown away by one of those wines. I think that's probably still the challenge for Chile, so much of what's being made is by the big guys and they aren't really focused on making terroir-driven wines.

If you were to draw a parallel with New Zealand: it produces a tenth of the wine that Chile produces, and there are 700 wineries. Chances are when you buy a wine from New Zealand, you're buying it from a very small producer who's going out there and starting off each day by saying in the vineyard, "What's the thing that we can do better than everyone else?" Whereas verbally, the big guys like the big players in Chile, or Gallo or someone like that in the States, they start off by saying, "What do people want to drink right now?" Then they go to their winemaking team and tell them, "This is the wine that is selling well in the UK supermarkets. This is what we have to make, in this style."

I think if you approach winemaking the wrong way like that, then the wines become bland and uninspiring. I already mentioned that in Chile, the great thing is these old vineyards. There's exceptional fruit here. There are amazing areas. There are whole valleys that haven't even been planted with a single grapevine yet, so who knows what's going to happen in five years?

Certainly since I arrived 15 years ago, Casablanca was new and exciting. Since then Leyda exploded, Limarí and Elqui have become wine producing regions. They have always been Pisco producing regions, but now they're well-known for wine. Bío Bío as a southern region. All these southern regions have started popping up. Atacama in the extreme north. There's just so much to do here, whereas I think if I look at New Zealand today, I feel as if New Zealand has done 80 percent of what it's ever going to do, and that's all been in the last 25 years.

Chile - I look at Chile and I think it's still maybe 30 percent of the way to where it could be in the future. There's a lot more that's going to happen in Chile. I think it's an interesting place for that reason.

How do you see the future of wine in Chile?

No idea. It's an interesting exercise I do every three years. I write the wine section for The Lonely Planet, the Chile guide. Every three years they get in touch with me and I sit down and I write what is essentially a two-page snapshot of what's happening in the Chilean wine industry right now. Every year I just write the vision for the upcoming guide. I write about completely different things every time because there's totally different stuff happening in the industry all the time. I think that's a real positive. It shows how dynamic the industry is, and how fast things can change. For example, six years ago I was writing about the explosion in quality of Pinot Noir, coastal Pinot Noir vineyards. And then three years ago, I wrote about sparkling wine starting to happen, and sparkling wine has just gone crazy here in the last three years. There's always been lots of cheap sparkling wine in Chile, but the move to making méthode champenoise, bottle fermented, serious sparkling wine has really just gone crazy in the last three years.

Apart from that, MOVI or the groupings of small independent producers, the "garagistes" if you like, that's gone ballistic in the last five or six years, has made the wine scene so much more interesting in that we have small players making these small batch wines from all over the country. País has been rediscovered as a grape variety, thanks to Miguel Torres down south. They didn't want País to disappear as a grape variety, because it was becoming extinct, so those guys grabbed País and started making sparkling wines and rosés. They make some really interesting wines now from País, all over southern Chile and by many different producers. The same thing with Carignan. It suddenly became a new thing, and there are some amazing wines being made out of Carignan.

Yeah, God knows what's going to happen. Natural wines already are starting to take off down south. I'm a little bit skeptical about the natural wine thing in general, because most of them aren't very drinkable, but once again, it's a counterpoint to the big guys. It gives people an alternative. I think it's really important that Chile starts doing new, interesting, different stuff. God knows, in three or four years, Tannat might be the new thing. Maybe Uruguay - we'll put them out of business and Tannat will be coming from Chile. Who knows? There are definitely a lot of different things going on right now, and I think with the appearance of all the new smaller players in the market, it just diversifies things so much more. I think the ball has started rolling, it's gaining momentum, and I think that's going to keep happening for the next five or 10 years at least.

Is there anything that you do that has changed from the vineyard perspective since you've arrived?

There's definitely much more of a focus on making wines that reflect the terroir. The skin contact thing and the whites are a big part of that, but also there's much more emphasis on vinifying every block separately to make different wines, because everything we make in this cool climate is a single vineyard wine. We make three different Sauvignons from this one vineyard, three different Pinots, two different Syrahs, and a couple of different Chardonnays as well. To be able to create three distinct wines from this one site, you need to be a lot more focused on the terroir, the different soil types and everything else. I think that's probably the main difference. The skin contact thing has been huge. That signified a very important change in the process there, but also just keeping everything separate. All these small barrel lots, everything fermenting away. It's a lot more work, but it increases blending options later on to be able to create wines that are completely different.

Viña Casas del Bosque
Hijuelas N° 2 Ex Fundo - Sta Rosa, Casablanca
Región de Valparaíso, Chile
Tel.: +56 2 2480 6940
Email: info_cdb@casasdelbosque.cl
www.casasdelbosque.cl

CESAR OPAZO
CALIBORO

Count Francesco Marone Cinzano, owner of Tenuta Col d'Orcia, one of the historical cellars of Montalcino, fell for Chile, and specifically, La Reserva de Caliboro in the Maule region. Cinzano, from the famous Cinzano vermouth family, bought Caliboro in 2005 committed to create wines that are true to the region. The estate produces two wines: a Cabernet, Merlot blend and a late harvest Torontel.

We talked to winemaker Cesar Opazo, who helped to establish the estate in 1996, about Maule, old vines, and the evolution of Caliboro.

Christopher Barnes: Cesar, tell us about Caliboro.

Cesar Opazo: Caliboro is a town in the Maule Valley, very rural, rooted in the colonial wine country of Chile, historical Chile.

And how is it historic?

As proof, in this area there are very old vines. Some older than 200 years. Some even more. Which shows how historic this area of the Maule region is.

Who owns the estate now?

The owner is an Italian man, Francesco Marone Cinzano, who established himself here with the goal of showing the origin of Chilean viticulture through innovation and the rebirth of this winemaking culture.

What has Francesco Marone Cinzano done to the estate since

he arrived?

He says that it was practically all here. That he didn't do anything but to rebirth this kind of viticulture with a concept of reviving the peasant tradition of Caliboro.

When did you start making wine here?

We initiated this project in 1996, starting from zero: we brought genetic material from Montpellier, France, to Chile; established the vineyards; cleaned the fields and planted the vines.

What is the philosophy of winemaking here?

The concept is very simple: one man, one brand, one wine.

Tell us about the different grapes that you grow here.

There's a genetic foundation here, it's the strength of the project. We're talking about Cabernet Sauvignon, Merlot and Cabernet Franc. But then we add Mediterranean varieties. Such as Alicante, Petit Verdot, Syrah, Barbera, Garnacha. That's an array that gives us the option and diversity to try and innovate the Chilean industry.

And how has winemaking changed over the period of time that

you began making wine here?

Very little. We are going back to the ancient tradition of winemaking. For instance, the handling of our viticulture. We don't water our vineyards. We aim for the best territorial expression of the area. There's great concentration on the grapes. We use native yeast for our fermentation. So we try to have a whole biological concept that's in balance with the environment, and with our wines.

Cesar, tell us about the organic viticulture here.

Our viticulture, organic or biological, is based on respecting the experience that the local people have. We are located in a place that's appropriate for this kind of viticulture. We are by the bank of a river, which allows us to have a thermic influence. We are in a place that has enough space, which helps us keep our vines healthy. So all we do is try to find the equilibrium in all this. So all the handling is based on the ancient style of viticulture, of pruning, of how they cultivated the vineyards in the traditional old way.

Tell us about Maule. What is the terroir that we are experiencing in this region?

The Maule, mainly in this part that we are now, has the most planted surface. It also produces a large quantity of grapes. There's a historical winemaking culture, so it makes me proud to work on this land because people have an experience inherited from their grand-parents and their parents in the handling of the vineyards. That helps us greatly in our aim to maintain this area in the traditional way. What makes the Maule different from the other valleys is that there's an intention to keep the tradition, especially in this area where we are now, which is the coastal dry interior of the seventh Maulean region.

Cesar, tell us about Torontel. It's a very interesting wine that you are making there.

The Torontel is recovered from an old colonial varietal, with the goal of reviving the tradition of a mass style of wine, historic in Chile. And the idea was to reuse these vines which are more than 70 years old and were abandoned. The goal is to position and show the Chilean industry an attractive wine - to give them a smile. And also to reflect the diversity of Chile with the rebirthing of these historical varieties which were lost, so to speak.

The grape already comes with a certain concentration, since the vines are not watered. And when we hang them, that facilitates a stronger concentration to the point that they dehydrate, lose their water and have sugar. And that allows us, besides having the concentration, to bring out the natural yeast that the cluster itself has. Therefore, we have a natural biological product which perfectly represents the land that it comes from.

You also grow País here. It's a very interesting grape that has been growing in this region for a long time. Tell us a little bit about that.

Our vineyard has always stood out for our idea of innovation, but innovation based on looking for varieties that have an origin. When there's an origin there's a local identity. And with the País varietal, we continue to test, to look for the best adaptability to present a wine that's an innovation for Chile. That's the idea, experimenting to find the best potential of these varietals.

Cesar, you've lived abroad, you were in Italy for some time and decided to return to Chile. Why did you make the decision?

Mainly, what makes me proud, is to search the origins. The identity. And I'm here from day one, soon it'll be 20 years working this vineyard. It is because what attracted me was the people, which is the main concept to look for in the local origin. Wine is not just made from grapes, but also with people, who also influence the success of a wine. And as a Chilean, as a Maulean, as a peasant of this region, that motivates me to maintain the peasant tradition.

Reviving the soil itself, working with my people, and making a product the world will know. A wine that will go from the Maule out to the world. Behind that bottle, there are people involved. Visiting Europe and other countries helped me realize that Chile has a diversity and a wonderful potential to show the world. And that's the objective I'm working on with my people here in Caliboro. Also with this Italian gentleman, who brings with him a European culture, and we have here an Andean Chilean Mother Earth. And that's the mutual respect that goes hand-in-hand to make a great wine in harmony.

www.caliboro.com
Email: cinzano@caliboro.com

RENÁN CANCINO
HUASO SAUZAL

Renán Cancino makes very traditional wine in a small town called Sauzal in the Maule region of Chile. He works with vines that are up to 300 years old.

We talked to Renán about traditional winemaking, the unique terroir of Maule and what is real natural wine.

Christopher Barnes: Renán, how did you get involved in winemaking?

Renán Cancino: Because of university, because of my profession. I studied agronomy in a university here in Chile. My first job as an agronomical engineer was in viticulture, in an agricultural producer's co-op, in 1997. That's where my connection to viticulture started, and now with wine, which was the next natural step.

And you work for a large company doing agronomy, but you've also decided to start your own wine label. What made you take that step?

I worked for several big companies in Chile, but there was also another inkling. My family produces grapes and when I was little, we made wine in our family, so there was always the urge to make wine. In the first stage, as an experimental wine for us to drink, and in the second stage, in 2008, 2009 and 2010, we tried to make a commercial wine. So there was a previous connection to wine, which then repeated when we started working.

Renán, what do you think of natural wines?

Natural wine is traditional wine. This project makes natural wines, not because of today's trend of natural wines that has taken over the world. But simply because that's the way wine has been made in Sauzal forever, since the start. Here they never used chemicals,

technology or preservatives. Therefore, wine in Sauzal IS natural in concept and origin. So what we do is a traditional wine, not a natural wine.

How is the terroir in Sauzal?

Maule, which is our region, is a very, very big region, with a wide variety of soils and climate. So to talk about Maule in general is complicated, there are many places of the world in Maule. Sauzal, in particular, is an area that has soils of a granitic origin. The whole coastal range, from Casablanca to the Nahuelbuta Range is coastal batholith. Basically it's granite soil, of a higher acidic pH, which gives a particular soil condition to the wines. And Sauzal, climatically, is in the valley but farther in the interior, closer to the coastal range, with a wider thermal variation and a stronger influence of the cold towards autumn. Therefore half of the summer, which goes from December to March, has more characteristics of autumn than summer. This is unlike the rest of the areas in the valley, where temperatures are more stable and homogenic until the end of the summer. So it's a naturally cooler area, it has a different climate condition. That, associated with the granite soils, makes very particular wines.

How old are the vines that you are working with right now?

We work mainly with three varietals. Two of them are ungrafted, such as País, which was one of the original Chilean varietals, planted when the Spaniards came to Chile. They may be 250 or 300 years old, we are not certain. Sauzal was founded in 1790 and many of these vineyards are very old.

The town elders knew these vines were already old, so they are really antique, centennial. Then we have Carignan, which is a variety that was incorporated into Chile after the 1939 earthquake, to improve the quality of common wines in this area. It's been 70 or 75 years since they were planted ungrafted, so it's also an old varietal, within context. And the third one we use is Garnacha, which we incorporated 10 years ago, but which we grafted onto old País vines. They are old roots. So all three varietals are very old, really ancient.

You spent quite a lot of time traveling around Spain. How has that influenced you as a winemaker?

In general, the influence of those wines and travels in how we make our wines, is none. What we do nowadays is ancestral enology. We make our wines as they've been made here for 300 years. And we don't do anything differently; we haven't changed a thing. I did miss a connection with the origins of Chilean wine. We descended from Spain and the first Chilean wines were led by Spaniards, and this area's viticulture is Spanish, so I was eager to learn what was behind that.

In general there were no big differences, just understanding that the south of Spain is the connection to Chile in terms of ancient viticulture, and the north of Spain didn't seem similar to what we do here at all. So I was more interested in understanding it rather than incorporating new technologies. What we do here is ancient viticulture and ancient enology. We haven't changed what's always been done here. We believe that's the way to work. So the way we make wines and the way we cultivate the vineyard, has, for me, the science of the wines that can be made here. Ultimately, every wine depends on the way the vineyard is cultivated. And that is really different here, compared to the rest of Chile and clearly with many other places in the world.

How has your winemaking evolved over time?

There has been no evolution. We were finally convinced that the wines we like best are the ones that were always made here. So we haven't modified anything, in how we handle the vineyard nor in how we make the wine. We haven't incorporated anything new. Here we do as it has been done for the last 300 years. And to me it's the natural component of the terroir that's abandoned everywhere in the world. Everywhere there's climate and soil, but there's no culture behind the wines, there's no history. They all make wines as they've seen them made lately, mixing everything with anything. Here we do exactly as always. And to me, those are origin wines. Wines from a place, that show a culture. And that's something I've rarely seen around the world.

FRANCISCO BAETTIG
ERRÁZURIZ

Errázuriz is a family-owned winery located in the far north of Chile 65 miles outside of Santiago. Don Maximiano Errázuriz founded Viña Errázuriz in 1870 and planted the first French grape varieties in the Aconcagua Valley. Today Errázuriz is managed by Eduardo Chadwick - the fifth generation of his family to be involved in the wine business. Chadwick has overseen many significant advances for Errázuriz including developing never before planted coastal areas, launching an icon wine, Seña, in 1997 to compete with the Bordeaux First Growths, and partnering with Robert Mondavi.

Winemaker Francisco Baettig started at Errázuriz in mid 2003. He has more than 1,000 acres of vines to work with in the cool-climate Aconcagua Valley.

Christopher Barnes: Francisco, tell us about Errázuriz.

Francisco Baettig: Welcome to Errázuriz. It's part of what we consider an old and classic winery. It was founded in 1870, so really it's been around a long time, but at the same time, it's a very unusual winery. Why? Because it's a family owned winery. The owner is a very energetic and involved person, a young person, with a passion for wine. He's always trying to maintain the heritage and the history of the winery, but at the same time, looking for new things, improving, and moving forward in every aspect. It's very attractive to work here because it's a link between the past and the future.

How did you end up at Errázuriz?

That's a good question. Faith, I guess. I started as a winemaker in Chile. All winemakers are agronomists, or agriculture engineers as I think you say. We start with agronomy and at some point, you choose

your specialization, the specialty you want to go into. I decided to go into winemaking because Chile has produced wine for many, many years, since the Spanish arrived in the 16th century. But the modern way, to export high quality with more technology, started in the beginning of the '90s, end of the '80s.

I've had to make my choice as an agriculture engineer. Chile was just starting to export, to improve quality, to have articles in the press about the new things going on. I felt it was very attractive, very interesting to be part of that rebirth and the new challenges for Chile in the wine industry, so I decided to go there. I started in other wineries, Casa Lapostolle, maybe you heard of it from Colchagua, where Michel Rolland was a consultant, so it was very interesting for me to be there. Then I studied in France, I did a master degree in Bordeaux. I met my wife there, and I kidnapped her. When I came back from France, I started in Errázuriz.

What would you say are your main influences as a winemaker?

I was influenced by Michel Rolland at Casa Lapostolle. He was very well-known and had a big influence on the wines he made. But then you start to try to find your own way. You take things that makes sense to you, and then you have your own evolution. Actually, in Chile, when we started this new development, in the beginning of the '90s, there were not a lot of winemakers. There were very few winemakers because it wasn't a very developed area in Chile, so a lot of young winemakers ended up managing a winery. At that time, we didn't really have a lot of experience, so you sort of follow a little bit what the market demands, or the consultant, and at some point, you start to find your own way.

Chile is very far away from all other countries, but Chileans began to travel, and to visit producing areas. Since we are so very far away, and it's very hard to find wines from overseas, we're all inspired to travel and visit the different wine producing areas like France, for example. That was how I started to be influenced, and my style also, from visiting France. I studied in France, and at some point, you find the style of wine that represents you, and that's when the evolution occurred for me.

Francisco, tell us a little bit about the terroir of Aconcagua.

Aconcagua is a valley north of Santiago, not too far, about 80 kilometers north of Santiago. It's a narrow valley. It's not as wide as Maipú, which is in the middle, around Santiago. This narrow valley goes from the coast, the Pacific Ocean, to the Andes, and it's shaped by the Aconcagua River. It's a very particular valley in that sense, because it goes from the Andes to the Aconcagua Coast, so it's a more restricted area, more central or coastal. It's a valley that has some influence on the temperature here. It's drier and slightly warmer than the classical Maipú, because we're further north, so it's very good for producing late ripening varieties in the interior part.

In Chile, the closer you get to the Pacific Ocean, the cooler it becomes because we have the Humboldt Current coming from Antarctica. And the closer you get to the Pacific it's cooler, and the more inland you move, you lose that influence of the cooling breezes from the Pacific, so you have warmth. In this valley, we have mainly rain in winter, so if you're inland, we have late ripening varieties. It's a very healthy valley in terms of disease, we don't have a lot of rain. As you move to the coast, you arrive at a cool-climate valley, so it's a very diverse valley, because we can go from extremely cool on the coast to extremely warm.

Here, it's moderately warm, so we can produce Cabernet. If you

continue to move farther inland, it becomes really warm, and we can produce Mediterranean varieties, like Grenache or Mourvèdre. It's a very interesting valley in the sense that in one valley, you can go from Pinot Noir, or cool-climate varieties to Mediterranean varieties in the same area. Then you have the diversity of soil that gives particularity to the wines. So, you have diversity of soil as well as climate. Really, it's a very particular valley because of its diversity.

Is there a grape that you feel is the star of this area, or do you feel there are multiple stars?

It's been a big debate in Chile if Carménère, for instance, should be the flagship for Chile, or if Cabernet is still the flagship variety. I think Chile has a big, big advantage which is its diversity. In my personal opinion, I don't think Chile should stick to just one variety or use

Carménère, the equivalent of Malbec in Argentina, or Sauvignon Blanc in New Zealand.

Chile is 40,000 kilometers long. If you had visited 10 years ago, or maybe 15 years ago, the producing area was going from the classic Aconcagua area, down to Maule. That's more or less 600 kilometers. Today, if you want to visit all places, you have to go 1,200 kilometers from Elqui to Traiguen, Malleco south. That's north to south, and then the diversity we've been developing in the last 15 years is from the coast to the Andes. In the Andes, we were very limited in development. Now you will find more and more vineyards there, and also on the coast. I think today, the challenge is to improve, fine-tune the style and the quality of the wines. We can produce a very attractive Chardonnay or Pinot on the coast, to very attractive Carignan in the dry farming area in the south, to a very attractive, I don't know, Grenache more inland and the classic Carménère. I mean, Chile is very particular in that sense with a diversity that I think we should explore more than one variety.

Francisco, Errázuriz is a very old company, and yet you're known for innovation. How did that come about?

We've had a lot of firsts. First to plant in the foothills with drip irrigation, first to bring all the varieties, first to create an icon or flagship wine. We carry many firsts. It's part of the DNA and goals of the owner, so it's very challenging, but at the same time, it's very attractive to work here. We have here, for instance, a Pinot Noir from the coast, from this Aconcagua Costa region. It is also a new area that was just planted in 2005, so it's a very new place, near the ocean, and a very exciting area for us.

Talk about some of the innovations that you've undertaken here.

We have many. We have an interesting project on the coast. I'm trying to, how to say, to access and to develop an appellation within these properties to handle 30 hectares, planted, with Pinot, with Chardonnay, cool-climate Syrah, and Sauvignon Blanc, with this particular schist soil. I think we have a very particular terroir that I'm trying to map in terms of style, and quality potential and then relate it to the wine, so we can create products that are closely related to the terroir, rather than just creating labels.

That's a very appealing project. We have done that with a Pinot, we worked with a French producer, she's well-known. Then I brought a geologist from Burgundy to help us to do all the mapping and divide the qualities or the style, like the Grand Cru. We won't use those names of course, but that's the concept, and it's an interesting undertaking that we're developing today but we have many, many others.

Francisco, tell us about the partnership with Mondavi.

Robert Mondavi came to visit Chile I think at the beginning of the '90s. Eduardo Chadwick, the president of Errázuriz, was very young at that time, and he was his chauffeur, so he moved him around, he contacted the wineries, and he showed him the different wine areas of Chile. They became friends, and then they started to talk about an idea, a project, and to create a joint venture, like he did with Opus One and to start developing Seña. Then in '95, they came here many times and founded the place which is now Seña, and developed, planted, and began to produce his wine.

Then Mondavi is sold to Constellation.

Yes. In 2004, it was purchased by Constellation, and Eduardo wanted to work with it, with the people, with the family, not with the corporation, so he purchased Mondavi's share. Since 2004, Seña wine is Errázuriz and Eduardo Chadwick owns the project.

Tell us a little bit about getting into the icon category. When you came out with your first icon wine, there were a few eyebrows raised. How did that happen and what has happened since?

I think it's understandable that people were surprised. Chilean wine was mainly known for entry level wines at, let's say roughly $10 a bottle, then suddenly the price jumped to $100 a bottle or $50 a bottle at that time for Seña. People were very surprised and I can completely understand it. Also, Chile started to export. Chile has always produced wine, and wine is widely consumed in Chile, but as a product in the market around the world, it was fairly new. People knew Chile by these entry level wines but not by this very expensive wine. I think it's something that we needed to create, maybe we went a bit too fast, we could have done it more slowly, filling the gaps step-by-step. The goal was to show that Chile had the potential for producing world-class wine. The terroir, the climate, all the conditions were there to produce fine wines. That was the point of these wines.

In terms of the Chilean wine industry right now, what are the biggest challenges it faces?

There are many challenges. If you realize that we only started to export wine, not produce, it's only been 30 years and the wine production is nothing, it's really nothing. I don't want to sound pessimistic, because really what we've done in the last 30 years is huge.

From not being in the market, now we're everywhere, the Chilean brand is known, but I think we have a big challenge in terms of moving up and moving away from this idea of good price, cheap good quality wine, which is difficult when you are set in one category, it's very difficult to move forward.

We've been consistently moving up and changing things, like paying more attention from the beginning, the plant material, the origin, the soil, the market, developing new projects, small projects. I think the fact that new players are coming into the scene is great, and we needed that, because that pushes the big guys and that also gives more sense of place to different projects, it gives more complexity, diversity to the country. I'm really optimistic in terms of what's going on. I feel that the winemakers, we are all there, and we're fine-tuning, and finding the style that represents us more. I think there are still many changes in terms of reaching the consumer, showing the new Chile, which is a reality today.

Today, that's the main challenge. I think we really have the potential, the terroir, the quality, all that, but we have to do more work in terms of communicating, reaching the market, reaching the consumer, but the quality and the style are going in the right direction, and Chile has become really more diverse in not just product, but also in producers. Chile used to be the least automatized producer in the world.

Internationally Chile is known for this sort of value, but inexpensive wine. There are a lot of very innovative things going on, which you're doing, but how do you get out of the mindset that associates you with these inexpensive wines and focus more clearly on the interesting things that are happening in the country?

It depends a lot on the market too, because if you go to Asia, for instance, where there's less preconception, and the consumer has less experience, so to speak, they are more open to trying different things. We do very well with our icon or flagship wine. We sell very well and since they try just the quality wine, we do very well. That's one thing market-wise. Then also all these new things, new wines that we're producing, what we need is for the consumer to just try the wines. When we show what we have done in the last five years, in Chardonnay, Pinot, Sauvignon Blanc, you name it, people are really surprised. They really think the wines are worth it and it is still a bargain. But we need to reach the consumer. That's a long-term challenge, but I'm very confident. In the last five years, the evolution has been very fast and very positive.

Okay. Francisco, where do you see the future of wine in Chile?

I don't know. I see huge diversity, and I see the consumer starting to really appreciate that. This is something that we need to create, but it's real. I really like the diversity because it provides more opportunity, you're not sticking to just one variety, you're reaching a more diverse consumer. I think Chile requires some structural changes in my opinion, such as working a bit more in the appellation system. That, for me is a little bit broad, or too loose. We need to promote specific places, or local areas.

We require some changes there, and we have to balance, as a wine producing country, reaching the consumer, but at the same time, to show more and more personality in the wines. Wines with a sense of place that are supported by a more formal appellation system, maybe not as complicated as France, but I think we have to work a little bit on that. I think the potential in terms of quality and style is huge, and we're just starting to feel more confident. When I make wine, I feel that I don't have to explain the wine. People try the wine and they appreciate the wine.

In the past, we were saying, "This is like this, this is like that. We want to be like this or that." Today, the personality of Chile is starting really to show, so I think it's a bright future, but with a lot of work, of course.

You're not of the opinion that Chile should stick the flag in the

ground for Carménère.

Not really. I think Carménère is interesting to have as a signature variety, or variety that you can identify, a little bit like ours, but I think it would really be a mistake to stick to just one variety. The quality potential is huge in many varieties and that's Chile. Chile's diversity is long, 40,000 kilometer long, from the coast, Andes, north, desert, lakes, et cetera, so we really need to touch on that, and to do that.

Viña Errázuriz
Av. Nueva Tajamar 481
Oficina 503 Torre Sur
Las Condes, Santiago, Chile
Tel.: (56-2) 2 339-9100
www.errazuriz.com

FELIPE TOSSO
VENTISQUERO

The Ventisquero winery was founded in 2000 in the Maipo Valley. Ventisquero currently has seven vineyards in the major growing regions throughout Chile. The diversity of climates allows Ventisquero to produce a variety of wines each with a unique expression of Chile's distinct terroirs. In 2004 Ventisquero and Tosso partnered with former Penfolds winemaker John Duval to develop the Pangea Syrah range from the Apalta region.

Grape Collective talks to winemaker Felipe Tosso, who has been with the estate since its inception.

Christopher Barnes: Felipe, tell us about Ventisquero.

Felipe Tosso: Our first vintage was 2001. We planted a little bit earlier. We started in 1996 with the project. It's owned by Gonzalo Vial. Just one owner. Private owner. We have several vineyards planted from Casablanca, Leyda, in the Maipo Valley, and here in Apalta, where we are right now.

What is the philosophy of winemaking at Ventisquero?

I would say that we only grow our own grapes today. One of the things I say is, "We are terroir-driven wines." That means there is a lot of common sense in the wine, not too much winemaking, really. We try to let the grapes express in the glass. Not a lot of filtration, or no filtration sometimes, depending on the level of the wine. Really concentrating on getting a more gastronomic experience with the wine, so all the winemakers work together. We work with our partner John Duval, our wine consultant, and some of our partners, on making wines that you can drink with food.

Because of that, we don't do super big wines. We're much more

focused on elegance. On nice tannins. On complexity in the wines. Earthiness. We like to take out the flavors of the earth. Sometimes our wines are not perfect. They're not polished, exactly, but they're nice to have with food. That's a very important part of the way we make wine.

John Duval, he was the head winemaker at Penfolds for many years. I'm assuming he's making Syrah here.

The one that we have right now is a blend of Grenache, Carignan, and Mourvèdre. In Spanish we say, "Garnacha, Cadinena, y Mataró." We do Carménère together also. We do a blend of Carménère and Syrah. We do, of course, a straight Syrah. Here in Chile it's Syrah, in Australia it would be Shiraz. So we do Syrah in Chile, not Shiraz. But he's a red winemaker mainly.

How did John Duval adapt to Chilean terroir as somebody who has been making wine for so many years in a very, very specific place?

I think you have such a talented winemaker. The first thing is that John is not bringing a recipe. The first thing he will tell you with his words will be, "I don't bring a recipe to Chile." The first is trying to understand Chile. Working together. Using our Chilean winemaking methods, and of course learning from him. We've been working nearly 12 years together. It's a long time. I go to Australia and he comes here.

Just to put it in perspective, John has never, ever made a cold maceration. We always do cold maceration. He doesn't need it; we like it. He doesn't do very long skin-contacts in Australia; we do from three weeks up to six weeks of skin-contacts. There are a lot of differences, but it's like cooking to me. To me, to be a winemaker is very near to being a cook. There's a way that you like to eat, and that system together ... we connect very well together. We like food; we cook together, and then the winemaking is about having nice tannins. Having elegant wines. Structured wines that are firm, but are also beautiful aromatically. There's a philosophy of winemaking that we have that is very similar. In a certain way I chose him as a consultant winemaker, and he chose us, saying, "Okay, I'll work with you guys. You have something I would like to work with. I think it is something exciting." We try to make exciting wines.

Felipe, tell us about your background. How did you get involved in wine, and what was that "ah-ha" moment when you knew that you were going to be a slave to the grape?

Look, I was very good at math, which has nothing to do with winemaking. I said I was going to be a civil engineer like my dad. Then I had the luck to live in Davis when I was very small, from five to 10 years old. Beautiful sky. The fields were nearby; it was a countryside area.

When we came back to Chile, I was 10 years old. I thought, "There is a little more smog in Santiago. A little more pollution. I don't want to live in Santiago." Then I went to university. After two years of studying civil engineering I said, "I'll have to work in buildings, offices. I want to live in the countryside." So I changed my career to study agronomical science. Once inside this field of study I discovered winemaking. I found it fascinating. I went to some tasting classes. Before, I always wanted to do that. A little bit of the artistic part. A little bit of the sensory part. You can feel things. But it also has a lot of science.

Today, I use the science aspect of it when we have problems, but to me winemaking really involves a lot of intuition. It's a lot like painting. There's a science to painting. There's a technique. But when you get freedom from that - the technique - you just go for it. That's how I feel after 21 years of making wine.

I have had been lucky to travel a lot, so I had a lot of work before in Concha Y Toro. Beautiful winery there. I learned a lot there and made good friends. Then I went to a smaller winery, though we have been growing bigger over last 15 years. But, I love the countryside way of

life. The connection to the land and to the earth, to be able to see the sky like today that is always blue and no pollution, a little bit of wind - that's what connects me to winemaking.

Felipe, how many different varietals do you work with right now?

We work with 12 different varietals. But mainly five reds and two whites. But the main thing is Cabernet and Carménère. Also Pinot Noir is getting very important, and so is Syrah. Those two, Pinot Noir is maybe second. We also have Merlot of course. Then we have a little bit of Petit Verdot, Cabernet Franc, and some other varieties that we are trying. We've had a little bit of Sangiovese, things like that. But the main thing would be Cabernet, Carménère, and then the second choice would be Pinot Noir and Syrah.

But of course in this area there are some Mediterranean varieties that we have planted recently, about five years ago. We have some Grenache, some Carignan, and some Mourvèdre. Spanish varieties that are used a lot in the south of France and in Spain. With the weather here it works very, very well, especially here on these hillsides. That's mainly on the reds. As for white wines, I would say we are very classic, so Sauvignon Blanc and Chardonnay are the main varieties. We have a little bit of Pinot Gris, a little bit of Viognier, some interesting things. But mainly Chardonnay and Sauvignon Blanc.

Sauvignon Blanc is big in this country today. I would say that after Cabernet Sauvignon and Carménère, our third most sold variety is Sauvignon Blanc.

How has your viticulture and winemaking changed in the time that you've been making wine here?

I think it hasn't changed a lot. I think we were lucky to plant in 1998, when there was a lot of expertise and research going on. There were a lot of studies of terroir. Then maybe 10 years later, or eight years later, we did a big study about soils.

Today, after years of planting, the things that didn't work we're changing. We're rethinking. For some things we're using some very good new clones. Everything that we do we trial first, so we plant half a hectare, and we see after four or five years if it works. Or we go and see our neighbor who has something good. We don't plant just because it's in fashion. It takes time. After 17 years we have been rethinking. We had a hillside where we had some Merlot; but it was too warm for Merlot. Merlot doesn't like so much heat. We already planted another part of it with a little bit of Grenache. It's similar soil so we're going to plant a little bit more Grenache.

So in general, like this farm that was a little bit more Cabernet-driven, today it is becoming a more Mediterranean style of vineyard for red wines. A little bit more Grenache. Syrah is very important. Some Carménère is important. I think we are rethinking some things that we have done before.

In terms of the Chilean wine industry, what do you see as some of the challenges that it's facing right now?

I think one of the big challenges is to be able to show people we are well-known to be producers of good value wines, but we are more than that. I think people need to appreciate that there's a lot of interesting stuff going on from our old vines to new plantings, to more extreme areas. We need to show people the diversity of Chile. From the north to the south, from the coast to the Andes mountains, there are a lot of small things happening.

Normally we see the big mass production type of things that people are able to get. How do we show the small producers of wine who are much more interesting than the massive wine producers? I think that's a big challenge today. We talk about industry, but this is not really an industry. How do we show that we're real farmers? There are people on the back of our wine, not factories of wine, really. I think that's the way to show Chile, more and more. Do you see this? You don't see any factory. There's no noise. Just some birds. This is what we work on. Making real wine. I think that's the other side we have to show.

You will be soon in the south of Chile, and you will see the real people picking things for us. You will see people picking grapes. The real workers are real Chilean people. They have small pieces of our vineyards. I think the modern part with the old part, but small productions of good wines with character. Not just a commodity. I think that's the next step for Chile.

Some people talk about Carménère as the grape of Chile, and some people talk about Cabernet. Do you feel that Chile should stand behind one grape, or do you feel that Chile should represent multiple varietals?

I think the most important variety in Chile is Cabernet Sauvignon, but it is not unique. We have to keep doing it well, because people like to drink Cabernet Sauvignon. It is a challenge to make Cabernet Sauvignon outside from all over the world, also from Chile. But there's some beautiful Cabernet Sauvignon also from Chile. Amazing. To just be focused on one variety - to me as a winemaker - I think is boring. I love to do different things. Maybe if you're in an area just devoted to Cabernet Sauvignon, maybe you will be more focused and do it better, but I love the diversity here. One day I can do a Carménère that I harvest in the last days of April. Then I can harvest Pinot Noir in the middle of March in the cooler area.

We have to be more original. From some areas, these are the best varieties. In all the important wine countries in Europe you don't see just one variety. In the north of Italy you cannot do what you do in the south of Italy. It's completely different. Chile is a little like that also. So the diversity will come more and more. Today, I think we are maybe too concentrated on Cabernet Sauvignon. There's Carménère, but I don't think it will ever be, "This is our flagship." Of course it's unique from us, but I think we are still quite a young country in terms of our activity now. We're an old wine country with 500 years of history, and we are recuperating some of our old stuff. I think that part is fascinating, but there's also new stuff coming.

All that diversity makes it interesting. Maybe it's not so easy to communicate outside, but it's what's happening right now. A lot of things are happening. Some people planted a little bit of Riesling on the mountain. Amazing. There's only one guy. One day maybe you'll have 20 guys doing that. Diversity is the thing about Chile. Chile is a very diverse country with its mountains, hillsides, flat areas, rivers, and coastal areas. That diversity of soils and terroirs make it a diverse area to plant different things.

One of the challenges with wine in Chile, in terms of the international perception, is that a lot of inexpensive, low quality, value wines were sold in Chile in the '90s. People began to associate Chile with that type of wine. How does Chile change the perception internationally, and show people the interesting things it's doing, and the different climates and wines that are coming out of these different areas?

It's a thing that nobody has the magic answer to, because that's what I have been talking about for the last 20 years. The only thing to do is at least travel the world and show what you're doing. I think sommeliers today are key. People who know: journalists, media. Go to everything. I think there is a world of that.

But that is also happening for a lot of other countries. You see Spain doing that, you see a lot of other countries. It is important that Chile keeps doing good value wines, because that's what sells on the normal shelf at the supermarket, but there's a lot of need to promote the small growers. To have the knowledge is very important to be important to your country. Our people drink more Chilean wines in more quantity, in more diversity. Not just the classic ones.

How do you get that word out?

Today, as winemakers, we're not just hard workers in the winery anymore. We're communicators. To communicate is a thing that is a must today for us. If you want to go outside, you have to speak English. You have to go outside. You have to know the people; you have to know the journalists; you have to know the media; you have to know the sommeliers; you have to go to restaurants. You have to get outside.

To me, wine is about people. When I go to buy wine in a wine shop, I ask the guy, "Which wine do I buy? Tell me the story of that wine." I buy wines with a story on the back as often as I can. To me it represents a way like a painter, like a movie, like a singer. When you go to a winery, it's not just the packaging. It's why do they do the wines in that way? There's a story on the back.

It's not so easy with just a label. We try to show things with a label, but sometimes the label doesn't say who you really are. But when that doesn't happen, you have to go outside and show your wines and show what's happening. It takes time. You have to know it will take maybe the rest of your life to change that.

I like to do good wines, and I like to go outside and communicate. I spend like three months traveling just to communicate, and I think a lot of my partners do the same. It's the only way. Get out there. Bring more people. Go there.

In vintage time, I receive two twice a week. People from all over the world. I tell them, "Bring them in vintage." They come and work with me. I say, "I go to Apalta, I have to go and taste the grapes." They come and taste the grapes with me. I go to the winery; they ferment with me. They are part of my work, so I consider it still work, but they understand what we're doing.

It's the only way: show, show, show. The more Chileans travel outside, the more Chileans show our wine, the more partners we have in other parts - in China, in the States, in Canada and Brazil, wherever – the more people would love Chilean wine.

Tell us about the terroir in Apalta.

Well if you just see how dramatic these hillsides are, and we have terraces and a big mountain over there, and a place where we have very old vineyards - downstairs there are some growers, they have some vineyards that are over a hundred years old, plus these here are new vineyards in the hillsides. When you see the colors of a vineyard, and the soils, that shows you that you have different soils. A lot of soils that sometimes just in 10 feet change completely.

It makes it very challenging as to which varieties are in what place, but because of the hillsides, not all the hills are good for planting. That's one thing. Everybody says, "Oh, all these hills are amazing." No, not all the hills are good. The hills that are good have a beautiful thing. First they restrain the vineyard so the vineyard grows slowly. They have good drainage. Chile has very good granite. There's a lot of quartz and iron, and some red clays that are very interesting.

The red clays and granite here, and a lot of stones and gravel, make it a very interesting soil, because you can have a little bit of clay that gives a little bit of power to the wine. But you also have the minerality of the granite, and that makes this a very beautiful area. But it's not a cool area, it's a warmer area. You really have to have red grapes. You need varieties that love sun. I think that's the beauty of Apalta.

VIVIANA NAVARRETE
VIÑA LEYDA

Viña Leyda is a pioneer in creating cool-climate wines in Chile. Leyda planted the first vineyard in the Leyda Valley in 1998. Prior to their arrival, the Leyda Valley, which is 12 kilometers from the coast, had been an area of pasture and basic crops such as wheat and barley. The valley is situated along the central coast of Chile and there is a strong influence from the Pacific Ocean, which is cold due to the influence of the Humboldt Current. The major challenge in grape growing in the area was getting water out to the valley, and this required Leyda building an eight kilometer pipeline.

Leyda has been able to achieve an exceptional price to quality ratio with their wines. It has been described by Decanter Magazine as "one of Chile's finest producers, exemplary for its consistently rewarding cool-climate wines that offer outstanding value for money and wonderful diversity."

We talk to winemaker Viviana Navarrete about the Leyda Valley and the path of female winemakers in Chile.

Christopher Barnes: Viviana, tell us about the Leyda Valley.

Viviana Navarrete: Leyda Valley is one of the newest valleys in Chile. It exists since 1998, and it's something really special. There was no viticulture here before; only dry pasture. The reason is that there is no water available. Irrigation is the issue as normally we receive only 250 millimeters of rainfall a year. That's very little for cultivating vines.

That is the nice story about Leyda Winery, because we are a pioneer in this valley. That's why our vineyard carries the name of the valley. We saw the potential of the soil and the climate, and we decided to make a big investment, together with the government, to bring water from the Maipo River to irrigate the plants. That was 18 years ago.

Tell us about the terroir in the Leyda Valley. What makes it unique? Why did you go through all the trouble of creating an irrigation system to grow grapes in this area?

Well, the fantastic thing about this place is this climate, which you're experiencing right now. We have a lot of morning fog from the Pacific Ocean, which is four kilometers from here. What you are experiencing right now is unusual in Chile. We have all the ripening processes of the grapes with this morning fog, so the grapes ripen very slowly, which is the best for cultivating Sauvignon Blanc and Pinot Noir. As a result, you get grapes with a high content of natural acids, low pH. The wines are really expressive and mineral and elegant, because of the influence of the ocean.

The other important element is the soil. We are on the west side of the Chilean Coastal Mountain Range. The soils are the oldest in Chile. We have granito, but we also have a lot of red clay that is very important. For example with the Pinot Noir, it's the red clay that gives you the mouth feeling and the creaminess. We have granito in the profile. Some spots of calcium carbonate that we have identified and those blocks we use for making special Sauvignon Blanc. In particular, because we are so close to the river, we have a lot of alluvial stones. We have a lot of different soils, and the nice thing is that here we are able to work in micro terroirs. We have separate blocks of small units, so everything is made very artisanally, very focused, by separating everything.

What grapes grow well in the Leyda Valley?

Well, that's a very interesting question because generally Chile is well-known for cultivating everything, anywhere. That happened early in the '80s. Nowadays, you can see that the wine industry people are getting more focused in what nature gives you. In that way, Leyda Winery saw the potential of this place, and we cultivate grapes that grow well in this kind of climate. Here there's no Carménère, no Cabernet Sauvignon, no Merlot; but we're have a strong focus on Pinot Noir and Sauvignon Blanc. Actually 75 percent of what we produce is between these two grape varieties. We also make Riesling, Chardonnay, Sauvignon Gris, and a little bit of Syrah, in a cold-climate style of Syrah.

Are all the grapes that are grown here used for your estate wines? Or are there growers in other parts that you use as well?

At Leyda Winery, we use only grapes from our own plantations. We

actually own 180 hectares. Anyway in this valley, there are some wineries and producers that sell grapes to other wineries as well. The interesting thing to know is that when we arrived 18 years ago, we were the first ones here with 90 hectares planted. Now you can find 2,000 hectares planted in the whole valley. That shows the great potential that this place has, because it has grown very fast. The interesting thing is that it's still a small valley, and it would be very difficult to grow further, because the price of the land has increased crazily. I would guess that it will stay a small and boutique valley in the future.

Tell us about Leyda Winery.

Well, Leyda Winery started colonizing this valley in 1998. It started as a family business. Nowadays, it's owned by the CCU Group. It's part of the VSPT Wine Group. Anyway, we work very separately as a premium and boutique winery. Actually we make three different brands. We have our Reserva level, the Single Vineyard, and the LOT category. Everything is premium, and we make about 33 different styles of wines. All from these cold-climate varieties.

How did you get into the wine business?

No one in my family is related to this industry. I started studying agronomy. Here in Chile you have to study agronomy to be a winemaker. I studied at the Catholic University. The last year of school you have to choose your specialization, and I chose winemaking.

Chile is still a bit of a difficult place for women to work; but winemaking is a fantastic area for women to develop. In the '90s, the wine industry was developing rapidly, and Chile was starting to produce more premium wines. Before, it was all about cheap wines and red wines, but something interesting happened in the early '90s. I saw that this was a huge field that was interesting to me, and as a woman, of course. Then I started working in a big winery for about six years. And then I ended up in Leyda as chief winemaker for eight years. I'm really happy here!

Tell us about women and wine in Chile. Are you seeing more female winemakers? And how many female winemakers are there?

Women are still lower in quantity compared to men. But every year women are entering the industry and able to make chief winemaker status. You can see in some wineries that women are getting into the chief marketing department as well. There are two general managers who are women. I think we fit very well in this arena. Especially in winemaking. It's not that women's noses are better, or they have more sensibility, many people say that; but I think it's that we offer a different kind of winemaking. Oftentimes journalists or customers try our wines and say they sense that they are made by a woman. I don't know if I am able to show that, but what I want to show to the consumers is a reflection of the terroir in the wines. I want the consumers to close their eyes when they try a Leyda wine and say, "Oh, this is cold climate, this is very mineral." I can feel the salinity of the cold-climate area that you are feeling right now. That's my main target. If I can make it better because I'm a woman, that's terrific.

What are some of the challenges the Chilean wine industry has been facing recently?

Actually, the Chilean wine industry is trying to show that Chile is not all about Carménère and Cabernet Sauvignon. This country is well-known, outside in the world, as a cheap wine producer with good quality wines. But I think that since the late '90s, winemakers have had the challenge to show that Chile has quite a lot more to offer. We have a very long coast, and we are discovering new valleys as this example in Leyda; but the same is happening up north and in the south as well. Also up in the Andes Mountains. We are trying to show the outside world that we have a lot more to offer, and to show high quality wines as well from different valleys and different grapes varieties.

You make three different types of Pinot Noir: the Leyda Range, the Single Vineyard, and the LOT. Tell us about the differences between those different wines.

Okay. In the Leyda brand, we are trying to show the consumer a Pinot Noir that is very honest and pure. For this wine we take grapes from different blocks and different exposures. Remember that Leyda Valley is everything about small, running hills facing to the north, to the west, everywhere. We pick grapes from different exposures, different clones as well. We actually have the 777, 115, clone 9, clone 16. Respecting the characteristic of each clone, we try to make a very expressive and fruit-driven style of Pinot, with very little oak. We want the consumer to feel the red cherries, the freshness, the spices that are typical from this region. It's a very friendly Pinot. Very juicy with a sweet texture, it's completely dry. It's a really nice wine for consumers that already know everything about Pinot, but also for people that are just beginning to learn about Pinot. It's a really nice wine.

Then for the Single Vineyard brand, we have two Pinots. One is called Las Brisas and the other one, Cahuil. They are more focused on the terroir. Here we make two different Pinots that depend on the soil. The Cahuil has a lot of red clay in the soil, so it's much cooler and has a high density on the palate. It faces north, so it's little more of a dark fruit profile.

Then we have the Pinot Noir in the vineyard Las Brisas, that is taken from two blocks that face south. It's a little bit cooler, and the soil has a lot of granito, so it's more vibrant and fresh. Many people say that Cahuil is a little bit more masculine and Pinot Brisas is more feminine, but it's nice to show two different characters of Pinot taken from the same vineyard.

Then we have the LOT Pinot Noir that is taken from a section of only one hectare. In a small hill, we have selected the upper part because we have a lot of calcium carbonate in this place. We select the clusters, we select the berries, everything is done in open steel tanks with a punching down regime, and here we use very little oak. Actually we're working with cement tanks and these big casks with no toasting. The idea is not to over deliver oak or chocolate or tobacco, but to show to the consumer the potential, the terroir, and the nice fruit profile that we have here.

You farm sustainably. Why is that so important?

Well, we have the philosophy of respecting not only the terroir, the soil and the plants, but the environment as well. We are very compromised with the produce that we use, we try to use as little as we can. We're actually working some blocks organically. I think our main enemy in this fog is the botrytis, but everything is made with a lot of conscience and not overusing products that can affect the ground.

Also we're committed to the community of Leyda, so we talk with people who live here. We're actually helping them to build a facility for the people. It's our philosophy to respect the place. We cannot come here and produce wines and sell cases; we also have a commitment to the environment.

This valley was planted in 1998. What have you learned about managing the vineyards since you started working here?

We have gained a lot of knowledge during that time. As you mentioned, we started 18 years ago with no knowledge, so the first plantations were made in a very traditional way that normal vineyards are planted in Chile. That means everything north to south, as far as the orientation of the rows, with density plantation of 3,000 plants per hectare, using the normal clones that we had at that time in Chile. Afterwards when we realized the potential and the quality of the grapes, we changed our thinking. We said, okay, we have to go into high-density plantation and completely change the design.

When we bought the next vineyard we made a huge investment in soil, in soil research, making five holes and five pits per hectare. At the end we had 500 holes in 100 hectares. It was the only way to really understand the profile, what's happening underneath, and to make a very good design of families of soils with different irrigation management. Then we went to the high-density plantation. We have some blocks with up to 10,000 plants per hectare, because we understood that here we have to talk, not of how many kilograms per hectare you produce, but how many kilograms per plant.

We played with the different orientation of the rows, because we understood that we have this problem of fog and it was very good to have some orientations east to west to use the breezes from the ocean as a tool in our vineyards. To allow the breezes to go through the rows. We invested a lot in clones as well. Actually we have nine clones for Pinot Noir and eight for Sauvignon Blanc, and that is only because of our experience. We now have a very well-designed plantation, and of course we are working with grapes that we really like that give good quality in this cool-climate area.

Leyda
Avenida Vitacura #4380, Piso 6
Vitacura, Santiago, Chile
Tel.: +56 (2) 477 5300
www.leyda.cl
@LeydaWines

40161731R00063

Made in the USA
San Bernardino, CA
13 October 2016